CW01486546

Murder, Suicide o

Bernard Knight

© Bernard Picton 1971

Bernard Picton has asserted his rights under the Copyright, Design and Patents Act, 1988, to be identified as the author of this work.

First published in 1971 by Robert Hale & Company.

This edition published in 2016 by Endeavour Press Ltd.

Table of Contents

ONE — THE DOCTOR AND THE LAW

Every doctor, from the moment he qualifies, has legal obligations and soon comes into contact with some aspect of the law.

As soon as he becomes a "registered medical practitioner", which means that he is entered on the Register of the General Medical Council, he acquires certain privileges and certain onerous responsibilities. These responsibilities far outweigh the privileges, which are confined to the right to practise medicine in the commonly accepted sense. Any person — quack or charlatan — can call himself 'Doctor' and set up in practice, as long as he does not hold himself out to the public as being a 'registered' medical practitioner; however, he cannot prescribe many drugs, nor can he treat certain diseases nor sign official certificates.

The responsibilities are legion — every doctor has to tread warily through an ever-thickening forest of rules and regulations, especially in regard to the National Health Service and the drugs that it is his very 'privilege' to handle. Like the clergyman, he is also much more vulnerable to breaches of ethics and general behaviour — his standards of conduct must be greater than those of the general public.

The 'Four A's' to a doctor mean Abortion, Alcohol, Advertising and Adultery as these are the common causes of his being struck off the register, upon which depends his very livelihood. Not for nothing is the telegraphic address of one of the doctors' defence societies called 'Damocles'!

On a less personal plane, doctors come into contact with the law in varying degrees according to which branch of the profession they have chosen as a speciality. Family doctors may have little direct contact with the law except through an occasional coroner's case or treatment of some assault injury in their practice. A dermatologist — a skin specialist — may never have any dealings with the law, except possibly in a civil court in connection with a compensation claim for a dermatitis allegedly due to industrial negligence. A casualty officer in a busy city hospital is more likely to get involved in wounding cases, and a house-man on a neurosurgical unit will frequently be called by the coroner to give him information on fatal road accidents.

But all these doctors have one thing in common — they get involved with the law without *seeking* to do so — in fact, the great majority are most reluctant to get involved unless absolutely necessary. This is mainly because of the great waste of time involved and the antipathy of most doctors to the atmosphere of the courts.

There are only two classes of doctors who go out of their way to become embroiled with legal matters and these work hand-in-hand with the law enforcement authorities — in fact, such work provides all, or a substantial portion, of their daily bread.

The first, usually part-time medico-legists, are the police surgeons. Formerly, these had a function described exactly by their title; they were doctors to policemen and their families. Though this function still persists in a few places, the advent of the National Health Service has all but abolished this aspect of their work, and most police surgeons are exclusively engaged in assisting the police forces in the 'execution of their duties'. These duties revolve almost entirely around the two 'pleasurable sins' — drink and sex!

The police surgeons, who are virtually all general practitioners with a family practice, examine drunken drivers and females who allege that they have been sexually assaulted. A third, but less frequent duty is the examination of bodies found in suspicious circumstances, but this will be discussed later. Both their major jobs are difficult and not particularly pleasant. They also tend to occur, like most medico-legal events, at unearthly hours of the night.

Since the new laws on drunken driving, it is also the duty of the police surgeon to take blood samples from suspected offenders. The usual procedure is for a police officer, if he has reason to suspect a driver of excessive drinking, to take a breath-test at the road side or police station. If the test is negative, that is the end of the matter, but if the crystals in the tube go green — indicating that probably the blood level will be in excess of the legal maximum — then the driver must give either a blood or urine sample for analysis. The police surgeon is called and he makes a note of the apparent condition of the suspect. The old law relying on the 'drunken' appearance and capabilities is still in force as an alternative to the blood-level law, but the police now rarely proceed under this Act.

The driver must opt for a blood test or giving urine; if he refuses both, this carries the same penalty as a conviction. The doctor, if he is to take blood, uses either a syringe and needle to take blood from an arm vein, or he pricks the skin and takes some drops of blood into tiny plastic cups. In either case, three samples are obtained; one is for the main analysis, another is a reserve. The third is offered to the driver, in case he wishes to get a private analysis performed for his own defence. The other samples are sent to the nearest Home Office Forensic Science Laboratory and if the level of alcohol is found to be higher than 80 milligrams per 100 millilitres of blood, there is automatic conviction.

The examination of women, and especially young girls, who complain of having been raped or otherwise sexually assaulted, is often the province of the female police surgeon, or a woman doctor who limits her legal activities to this sphere. Like the clinical examination of drunken drivers, assisting the police in this delicate and difficult matter is a job which needs long experience. In sexual offences, there is a high proportion of fraudulent accusations against men, especially from the younger girls, who act from spite or fantasy. Some of the technical aspects will be described later in the book, but it should be remembered here that the general practitioners who volunteer for this particularly thankless task are to be greatly respected.

The police surgeon is sometimes called to scenes of violent and suspicious deaths as well as to cases of non-fatal injuries due to fights and other violence, especially amongst brawlers arrested by the police and who are bleeding all over the police station on a Saturday night!

This function in the fatal cases is a little complicated by the fact that the forensic pathologist is also called to the scene of such cases and their function overlaps. Nevertheless, the astute police surgeon, arriving on the scene before the pathologist and the rest of the 'madding crowd' of investigators, may well be able to get a better assessment of the time since death, especially if the arrival of the pathologist is delayed.

The other sort of medical specialist who voluntarily gets mixed up in legal matters, is the pathologist, about whose work this book is mainly concerned.

Again, there are several sorts of pathologist. The great majority are 'clinical pathologists' who work for the National Health Service in our hospitals. Another large group perform somewhat similar work in the teaching hospitals of the medical schools, with a triple role of teaching students, carrying on research and doing the routine tests on the patients in the hospital. All these pathologists may further specialise in particular topics, such as bacteriology, biochemistry, haematology (blood diseases) etc.; but the ones with whom we are mainly concerned go under the name of 'morbid anatomists', a rather depressing title which means those who study diseased organs and tissues.

The medical school 'morbid anatomists' are further sub-divided into two groups, by far the smallest of which study *forensic pathology*, the study of the legal aspects of pathology, which often extends into other branches of medicine, when it is then more accurately called 'forensic medicine' or 'medical jurisprudence'.

By now, we have sub-divided the original medical profession down four times to get to the forensic pathologists, so it will be obvious that he is a pretty rare bird — and getting even more rare, there now being only about sixteen full-time men in England and Wales to cover the medico-legal pathology of some 40 million people.

As the number of coroners' post-mortem examinations is around 100,000 per year, it is obvious that this tiny band cannot be responsible for the bulk of medico-legal work. In fact, some 80 per cent of the cases are dealt with by the hospital pathologists. This must be so, as, apart from the actual work-load, geographical considerations do not permit anything different, with the present siting of the full-time pathologists in widely spaced university centres. An arrangement has been built up over the years, where the 'ordinary' cases — that is, cases with no criminal or suspicious element attached — are dealt with by the National Health Service pathologists. These deaths include sudden natural causes, accidents, suicides etc., though admittedly, cases often start off as 'ordinary' and end up as more complicated. Frankly criminal cases and cases with some peculiar or suspicious twist, are referred to the nearest full-time forensic pathologist, who may have to travel long distances to visit the scene of the death and then carry out a post-mortem examination.

As the 'full-timers' are now so thin on the ground, in an increasing area, all deaths, criminal or otherwise, are being dealt with by the hospital pathologists. The development of this system has given rise to the term 'Home Office pathologist', which is used by Fleet Street with more enthusiasm than accuracy.

In former years, Sir Bernard Spilsbury was 'the' Home Office pathologist, but now the term means a pathologist approved in the provinces by the Home Office — and paid a ludicrously small retainer which just about keeps tyres on his car — who is appointed as a consultant to one of the Home Office Forensic Science Laboratories situated around the country.

This is an appropriate place to describe these laboratories. Until about the mid-nineteen-thirties, almost all the scientific aspects of crime detection was carried out either by pathologists or by specialist scientists in other fields, such as chemists, toxicologists or public analysts.

In all the great murder trials of earlier years, the scientific evidence will be found to have been given by doctors like Alfred Swaine Taylor, Pepper, Sydney Smith or Bernard Spilsbury, or by a toxicologist like William Willcox.

Though criminology laboratories had existed on the continent of Europe since the early years of the century, it was not until 1935 that the Metropolitan Police Laboratory was set up in London. This laboratory was the product of co-operation between the Home Office and the police force and soon other laboratories were established in the provinces. Others were added after the war and now there are 'labs' at Newcastle, Harrogate, Preston, Nottingham, Birmingham, Bristol and Aldermaston. There are two laboratories at the last-named place, one being the routine establishment for the Home Counties, the other a pure research laboratory for the development of new techniques. The ever-increasing work-load of the routine labs has made this development necessary, so that systematic research can be achieved.

There is another laboratory in Wales, at Cardiff, but in Scotland, where the Home Office's powers do not extend, much of the scientific work is still done by the medical departments, though the City of Glasgow police have a long-established laboratory and another on the lines of the Home Office series is being set up.

In Ulster, there is an excellent system of collaboration between the university and the Home Department, which has established a State Pathologist, and, in addition, there is a criminalistics laboratory administered by the Ministry of Commerce.

Details of the technical work carried out by the Home Office laboratories is described elsewhere; but, in broad terms, they perform all the non-medical work associated with crime investigations, with the exception of photography and finger-print identification, which is done by the police forces themselves.

The laboratories do not concern themselves with civil litigation; this being handled by private consultants and commercial laboratories. Neither do they advise or appear for the defence, though full access is given to experts retained by the defence who wish to examine material relevant to the case.

Every regional laboratory is self-contained and can deal with almost every problem, but there is a tendency for special interests to be developed at particular centres. For instance, the Cardiff laboratory has a world-wide reputation in the examination of documents for forgery and the identification of anonymous letters etc.; the Preston laboratory has a special interest in arson examination, and the Nottingham centre is acknowledged as the specialist laboratory in fire-arms examination.

The Home Office laboratories are staffed by scientists holding university degrees, usually in chemistry or biology. These experts are called 'scientific officers' and are graded according to seniority and experience. There are also non-graduate staff who do not present evidence in court, as do the scientific officers. There are also one or two police officers, seconded from police forces in the drainage area of the laboratory, who act as liaison officers; they keep the meticulous records needed for preserving the continuity of evidence and assist both detectives and laboratory scientists at the scenes of crime. The bulk of the Home Office laboratories' work is, of course, not murder; the investigation of theft, crimes of violence (especially sexual assault) and the estimation of alcohol in drivers form a great part of their work-load.

Returning to the pathologists appointed to these laboratories — formerly they were almost all full-time forensic pathologists from universities, but, as their numbers are dwindling, there are not enough to cover the country. Now hospital pathologists are being appointed, so that they now cover an increasing amount of the criminal work formerly dealt with by the medical school specialists.

As might be expected, London is by far the best provided with full-time medico-legal pathologists, having well over half the total number in

England and Wales. In addition, they cover the serious cases for the Home Counties so, as there are adequate facilities in the South-east, no Home Office appointees exist here, in the provincial sense.

This division of pathologists into the full-time forensic practitioners and the part-time hospital pathologists, has given rise to some unease and occasional embarrassment, but it must not be taken to mean any significant difference in medico-legal competence. Some of the most penetrating and expert forensic minds have belonged — and still belong — to the hospital pathologists when employed on legal cases, but it must be said that the majority of hospital specialists, while quite willing to deal with the routine cases of sudden death, accident and suicide, are reluctant to get involved with serious criminal cases. Again, the main factor is the long wastage of time and the inimical atmosphere of the court, with its tense climate and the possibility of long ordeals in the witness-box.

The duties of the full-time forensic pathologist comprise several different functions. He is invariably on the teaching staff of a university medical school, holding the appointment of a lecturer, senior lecturer, reader or professor. The last grade is becoming rare in England and Wales. The only remaining established 'chair' of forensic medicine was abolished in 1969 on the retirement of the last professor. Although there are three professors in London, these are *personal* appointments, created as a recognition of the individual merit of the holders. On the retirement of these professors, the chairs will revert to more junior status.

On the continent of Europe, every Institute of Forensic Medicine has a professor as its head, and this tends to be the case in Scotland, where there are two established chairs. The one in Edinburgh has been vacant for a number of years, though in fact it is the oldest in Britain, having been established in 1805. At present, the majority — if that word is appropriate to such a small band — are lecturers and senior lecturers. This is more a *grade* than an accurate description of their function, even more so than with most university appointments.

Due to the crowded curriculum of medical students, with new medical and surgical techniques jockeying for bigger shares of the available teaching time, the amount of tuition in forensic matters has been drastically pruned. During the last decade, almost all universities have dropped the subject from their examinations and the number of lectures has almost universally declined.

There is considerable justification for cutting out the finer details of criminal autopsy techniques for undergraduate students, most of whom will become general practitioners. However, in some places the more practical aspects of medical ethics, negligence, certification of death and all the para-medical administrative matters which come under the broad heading of medical jurisprudence have suffered from the decline in teaching. In this context, it is significant that some of the organisations which offer legal protection and indemnity against actions for negligence etc., have recently expressed disquiet about the falling standard of knowledge amongst newly-qualified doctors in this basic area of legal medicine.

The academic duties of the full-time forensic lecturer represent a very small fraction of his total working time. It can be measured in hours per year, if one excludes the more informal teaching that takes place in the autopsy room.

This last occupation takes up the greater part of his working time, consisting of the day-to-day cases performed for the local coroner. Few of these cases will be criminal in nature, but they represent the same type of work as is carried out elsewhere for the coroners by the Health Service pathologists.

The criminal cases will come at unknown and irregular intervals; their frequency varies greatly. Sometimes, a week or two will go by with nothing out of the ordinary, then two nights' sleep will be lost in succession and several hundred miles travelling will be necessary to visit some distant scenes of violent death. There are seasonal rises in criminal deaths; August and the Christmas-New Year period are the most obvious. Week-ends are also busier, and this and the festive season rise can largely be explained by the national drinking habits!

There is a noticeable geographical difference, too; apart from the low density of population in rural areas, some cities and zones seem particularly prone to violent crime — Glasgow and Tyneside are examples, though by no means the only ones.

This direct connection of the forensic pathologist with the investigation of crime is the one which meets the public eye, through the medium of the Press and television. There is a built-in fascination about murder that attracts almost everyone, as the sale of crime novels testifies. Thankfully, there is less glorification of the 'crime doctors'' appearances than there was years ago. With the change in court procedure, he figures less prominently, except in really outstanding homicide cases. The popular image of the doctor presented by the Fleet Street journalist is projected to the public as someone who deals with bloody murder from nine until five every day — the fact that he may not appear at an Assize Court from one quarter to the next, but spend his time in routine examinations of coronary thromboses and in pursuing some highly non-criminal research, never gets across; what is dull to the news desk is not news! One of the objects of this book is to fill in the details, not only of the more macabre aspects of criminal investigations, but of the other 80 per cent of the pathologist's working day.

TWO — THE ROLE OF THE DOCTOR IN THE INVESTIGATION OF DEATH

Before medical and scientific techniques used in the unravelling of suspicious deaths can be examined in detail, some appreciation of the relevant system of law and its administration is needed. The doctor occupies a small but central position in this framework of law enforcement — indeed, often the very mobilisation of an investigation is at his behest.

The function of a medico-legal practitioner is intimately bound up with one of the most hallowed of the English public offices — that of Her Majesty's Coroner.

In England, Wales, Ireland, many ex-colonies and in the majority of the States of the U.S.A., the coroner has for years been the corner-stone of the investigation of unnatural deaths. His jurisdiction — at least in England and Wales — has been drastically curtailed during the last century, but he is still a Crown officer with considerable power, though many consider the office an anachronism.

Scotland does not share in this system, her legal machinery in general being geared more to the continental stream of Roman law, rather than Anglo-Saxon.

The English coroner was one of the earliest recognisable Crown officials. There may well have been the equivalent of coroners in Anglo-Saxon times, but he certainly appears in records of the early Norman period, being given a boost around 1194 by Richard Coeur-de-Lion. Richard, being financially embarrassed by his recent costly ransom and his foreign wars, looked around for additional ways of refilling the Royal purse.

One method was the more energetic appropriation of the property of felons, who were hanged for almost every offence, petty or otherwise, and their goods confiscated for the Crown. The sheriffs were inclined to divert much of this barbaric form of income tax into their own pockets, so other officials were appointed to see that such forfeitures actually reached the Crown coffers.

These 'Keepers of the King's Pleas' — *custodes placitorum coronae* — soon became known as 'coroners'.

Not only was a felon's property taken for the king, but the actual object associated with the cause of death was confiscated — if a man was killed with a sword, that was appropriated, or if a cart ran over him, that was gathered in for the king. This forfeiture of death-dealing property — the 'deodand' — survived right into the nineteenth century, and one of the last deodands to be appropriated was a railway engine which had run a man down!

Though this original preoccupation with sudden death has survived at least 800 years, the coroner accumulated several other jobs, all with some mercenary aspect. He was obliged to investigate wrecks, fires, treasure trove, catches of royal fish such as the sturgeon and to banish felons who sought sanctuary in churches.

The only functions to survive to this day are death investigation, treasure trove and fires in the City of London.

Originally, the coroner had to collect a jury to enquire into a sudden death; he still does in certain circumstances, but in early days, they had to be people who knew something about the occurrence — in other words, they were really *witnesses*, rather than a jury. Nowadays, the very opposite is the case and the jury is supposed to be uninfluenced by any prior knowledge.

The modern coroners' function is to enquire into 'where, when and by what means' a person came to his death, and he is specifically forbidden to apportion blame except in very limited circumstances. It is for other courts in English law to convict another party of causing the death, as will be explained below.

At the present time — though the coroner's powers are at present under review by an Interdepartmental Committee of the Home Office — the coroner deals with a wide range of deaths, the majority of which never come to his court for an 'inquest' to be held on them.

In England and Wales, almost 125,000 cases were reported to coroners in 1968, out of a total of 576,000 deaths. Such cases consist of accidents — both traffic, domestic and industrial — suicides, murders, manslaughters, infanticides, deaths in prison or police custody, deaths during medical procedures or surgical operations etc. — but the great majority are due to natural disease, mainly heart attacks.

This last group forms the bulk of the coroner's case-load and comes about when a family or hospital doctor is unable or unwilling to sign an ordinary death certificate. If the death is sudden or unexpected, the doctor cannot 'sign it up' if he has not visited the deceased within the previous fortnight before death or if he is not certain of the cause of death. For instance, a woman may be 'under her doctor' for dyspepsia or a bad cough, but even if she drops dead in his surgery, he cannot issue a death certificate, as her death was unexpected and not likely to have been associated with her previous complaints.

These heart attacks and strokes form the biggest single type of coroner's case, and he will dispose of them either by questioning the doctor more fully, or more likely, order a pathologist to conduct an autopsy to determine the cause of death. In large cities, the proportion of post-mortem examinations ordered approaches ioo per cent, but in some rural areas it is still very low. Until a few years ago, one coroner's district sported the extraordinary figure of only 17 per cent! As several surveys have shown that the error between a cause of death given *without* an autopsy and that *after* autopsy is between 50 and 60 per cent — in other words, without a post-mortem, the guess is more often wrong than right — it seems extraordinary that such low rates should persist. The annual coroners' returns show that even now there are still many *inquests* held without a previous autopsy!

Superficially this may be justified by thinking that the cost of an autopsy is a waste of public money in, say, a road accident where the driver has been so badly injured that the cause of death is obvious to any layman. But later issues of insurance, negligence, and possibly even criminal charges against another driver may be vitally influenced by medical evidence of a heart attack, faulty vision, other natural disease etc., which would not be available if no post-mortem were performed. Many an apparent accident has turned out to be either a natural death, a suicide or a mishap precipitated by heart disease when the pathologist's report has been forthcoming.

Returning to the coroner's procedure — once he is satisfied that death is due to natural causes, he can dispose of the case without an inquest and the matter becomes a paper transaction. He is still obliged to hold a public inquest on suicides, accidents, industrial diseases, deaths in police custody, and the criminal triad of *murder, manslaughter, and infanticide,* but, paradoxically at first sight, his powers in the last group have been reduced almost to nothing.

If a murder occurs and a suspect is arrested and charged, the coroner can only hold a brief 'opening' of his inquest, at which evidence of identity is given and also the bare cause of death, so that an order can be issued for the disposal of the body. He is then obliged to adjourn indefinitely under Section 20 of the Coroner's (Amendment) Act, so as to allow a criminal prosecution to take place; eventually, he is notified of the outcome by the Clerk of Assize. Whether the accused is found guilty or innocent the inquest is never completed and the coroner plays no significant part in the affair.

This shows up the almost universal 'howler' in hundreds of detective novels, where the coroner is portrayed as holding a full inquest, with a jury, a day or two after the vicar is found dead in his study. In fact, this cannot happen in law!

There is a relatively rare occasion when the coroner can become more deeply involved in criminal cases. Where no person has been charged with causing the death, then a full inquest has to be held. When such a death occurs, the decision whether to prosecute any suspect lies with the Director of Public Prosecutions in London, who studies the documents on the case supplied by the police and decides on these facts. If he declines to advise a prosecution — because of insufficient or weak evidence — the ball is thrown back to the coroner, who holds an inquest with a jury. Very occasionally, his jury — either with his encouragement or against his advice — may bring in a verdict of murder or manslaughter against some person. Then the coroner has no option but to invoke his few remaining ancient powers in the criminal sphere and commit the person named to the next Assizes.

As the standard of proof required to get a conviction at the Assizes is very high indeed — even higher than that required to persuade the Director of Public Prosecutions — then it is not surprising that the acquittal rate of coroner's committals is very high. There are only a few such cases each year (six in 1968) — mostly committals for manslaughter when the 'D.P.P.' has declined to prosecute for dangerous driving under Section One of the Road Traffic Act. This vestigial power of the coroners is under review by the Home Office Committee, who will decide whether it is worth retaining.

Going back to non-criminal deaths handled by the coroner, he has the duty of inquiring into all deaths which do not appear to be natural after either the physician's opinion or the pathologist's examination.

As mentioned, these include accidents, suicides and certain deaths associated with medical treatment, especially where relatives express disquiet with the proficiency of the doctor in attendance. It is a convention, though not a law, that patients admitted to hospital who die within twenty-four hours are reported to the coroner. Deaths during an operation or under an anaesthetic or deaths shortly after such events, are also reported. Any suggestion of negligence on the part of doctors or nurses leads to a public inquest, when the air may be cleared of rumour. In all these cases, the evidence of an impartial pathologist is necessary to arrive at a just verdict. Where death occurs in a hospital, and there is any suggestion of surgical, medical or nursing malpractice, the pathologist chosen by the coroner is usually one from some other hospital or medical centre, so that there can be no suggestion of 'covering up' between friendly colleagues. The evidence of the pathologist, as with all scientific witnesses, is utterly impartial, whether he is working on a murder or an anaesthetic tragedy.

Though the coroner has the power either to hold or to dispense with an inquest in most of his cases, certain types of death *must* be followed by an enquiry in his court. These include all suicides and accidents, industrial diseases, deaths in prison or police custody, where death was due to self-neglect (alcoholism and drugs come under this head) and, of course, the rather anomalous situation in connection with criminal deaths.

Formerly a jury was required in all inquests, but now they are dispensed with in suicides and all non-transport or non-industrial accidents, except where the possibility of some continuing public danger exists. This means that the greater number of inquests are now held without a jury; as we have already seen that by far the greater number of coroner's cases do not require an inquest at all (only 25,000 out of 125,000 in 1968), it will be evident that the jury inquest forms a very small proportion of the total, being mainly road accidents.

The form of the inquest is straightforward and may take only a few minutes. Traffic and industrial deaths usually cause the most complicated and drawn-out inquests, apart from the few criminal deaths that end in committal. In the former inquests, there are almost invariably solicitors and even barristers representing various parties, as there may often be later civil actions in another court over questions of liability. Thousands of pounds may be involved in compensation and the lawyers are there to guard the interests of relatives of the deceased, the employers, insurance companies and other drivers, depending on the nature of the case. In industrial cases, one of H.M. Inspectors of Factories may sit with the coroner to assist him and to ask questions on his own account.

In these inquests where civil actions may be in the offing, the legal representatives do their best to squeeze out every drop of evidence favourable to the party they represent. Sometimes the coroner has to step in to control the proceedings, as his court is there merely to ascertain what happened and not to try to apportion any blame which falls short of a criminal act. He is obliged to direct his jury to this effect at the end of the evidence, as frequently an over-enthusiastic foreman will try to add a rider accusing some party of negligence. This is expressly forbidden and the only acceptable riders are ones drawing attention to some continuing public danger — for instance, a 'black-spot' road junction may be referred to and the coroner will announce that he will make representations to the Local Authority about the erection of some extra warning signs. Any other comments cannot be entered on the record.

Unfortunately, there is no such express ruling that prevents the coroner passing personal opinions; though fortunately rare, the autocratic, acidulous and sometimes insulting comments that he passes can do much psychological harm as well as cause personal offence. He is completely protected from actions for slander by the privilege of his court, but, as will be mentioned later in connection with infant deaths, these occasional outbursts can do irreparable harm to some vulnerable members of the public.

Returning to the verdicts of the coroner's jury, 'accidental death' is by far the most common. 'Natural causes' are usually filtered off by the pathologist in the earliest stage so that no inquest becomes necessary. Criminal verdicts are very rare, as already discussed, so that usually only the 'open verdict' and 'accident' are left.

The 'open' verdict is self-explanatory and is arrived at when insufficient evidence exists to arrive at any definite decision. Most of these are dealt with by the coroner sitting alone, except where suspicious circumstances exist. If the cause of death is unknown — usually because the body is too decomposed (even a skeleton) after a long period since death, then no verdict can be reached. Again, many border-line cases exist between accident and suicide — for example, where a body is found floating in the river, with nothing to say whether the deceased *fell* in or *jumped* in deliberately. In many cases, especially those associated with overdoses of sleeping tablets, there is no suicide note or other evidence of intent to help arrive at a decision; most coroners will give the deceased and the family the benefit of the doubt and return an open verdict rather than a definite one of suicide. This avoids the lingering social stigma and may assist in insurance and religious matters connected with the death.

'Accidental death' is the one most commonly uttered by the foreman of the coroner's jury — sometimes reluctantly, where there seems to the lay jury clear evidence of negligence on the part of some other person.

As already explained, unless a *gross* degree of negligence is proved, sufficient to bring in a criminal verdict of manslaughter, the only alternative is one of *accident*. These criminal negligence cases are rare, as they get filtered off into the criminal courts before the coroner has to deal with them. One notorious example was many years ago, in the case of R. *v.* Bateman, where a doctor caused the death of a woman in childbirth; he was so drunk that he mutilated the woman with obstetric forceps while delivering her baby and was found guilty of such gross culpable negligence that it amounted to manslaughter.

A verdict hallowed by time, but now falling into disuse, is 'misadventure'. It is virtually the same as 'accidental death', but no one seems to be able to differentiate clearly between the two. It appears to indicate some deliberate act on the part of the deceased which led to his death, rather than a pure act of providence. For example, if a man walked along a river bank, tripped over a tree stump, fell into the river and drowned, that would be a pure accident. But if he dived into the water, intending to swim, then hit his head on a submerged rock and drowned, that would be a 'misadventure', as his entry into the water was voluntary. The difference is so slight, often impossible to determine and so lacking in legal significance that the verdict of 'accidental death' is coming to be used for all such mishaps.

At present, there are 230 coroners in England and Wales, all but 15 being part-time officials.

A coroner must have either a legal or a medical qualification, and in London and a few large cities, he must have both. These latter coroners are full-time officers, but elsewhere most of the coroners are solicitors, only a few being doctors. It has always been a point of dispute as to the relative merits of a legal or a medical qualification. As the bulk of the case load is natural disease and much of the remainder concerns medical problems, it would seem logical to think that a full understanding of disease and medical techniques was preferable to legal learning, 90 per cent of which will never be called into use in the circumscribed field of coroner's practice.

The very survival of the coroner has been called into question from time to time, it being argued that the American, Scottish or continental system is far more efficient. The coroner certainly contributes very little to the investigation of sudden or unnatural death — the evidence he takes from physicians, pathologists, police and the general public rarely leave the verdict in doubt, especially after a post-mortem. He merely rubber-stamps the decision and all the 'leg-work' is done by his 'coroner's officer', usually a police officer on permanent assignment to this work.

If the coroner's remaining powers of committal are removed, only the inquest remains as any justification for his continued existence. In the eyes of some critics, the inquest is undesirable anyway. A radical shift of medical and social opinion on suicide in recent years had made the public inquest into these deaths even more unpopular. Since 1961 suicide is no longer a crime and is universally recognised as a manifestation of mental disturbance, as much a disease as pneumonia and with no more moral stigma. The inquest on a suicide achieves nothing except distressing publicity for the relatives and leads to the publication of methods of self-destruction which have sometimes led to the imitative fatal actions of other suicidally-inclined persons.

Thus in some quarters it is felt that the only useful function of the coroner is in the investigation of public dangers like road accidents, industrial hazards and in rumours of negligent treatment, where ventilation of the circumstances in public may clear the air. Yet tribunals of traffic and industrial experts already in existence could probably deal more efficiently with the former cases. Medical negligence, if well founded, will, in any case, be dealt with by the civil courts.

Be that as it may, the rather diffuse function of the present-day coroner is one which is difficult to dislodge, mainly because no one feels strongly enough to devise adequate alternatives, though the medical examiner system of some States of the U.S.A. would appear to be the most obvious choice.

THE MEDICAL EXAMINER SYSTEM

In the United States, sudden, unnatural, or criminal deaths are dealt with by a coroner or by a medical examiner, according to the system employed by the particular State. The American legal machine was inherited from England, but has undergone profound and tortuous changes. The coroner system was universal until relatively recent times, but the American coroner is very unlike his English counterpart. In England and Wales, that official is appointed by a local authority when a post falls vacant and lasts for life or until retirement; there is also the requisite legal or medical qualification.

In the United States, a coroner's appointment is usually purely political; he is a nominee of a party and runs for office at every local election. His fortunes as coroner depend on the ability of his party to stay in office and he loses it when they are defeated. He need have no knowledge at all of law or medicine, and, in fact, a large number of American coroners are undertakers, where their business obviously profits from their official position.

The system is open to much abuse, and gradually the medical examiner system is being brought in, often against vigorous opposition.

The medical examiner is a doctor with specialist qualifications in forensic pathology. He is usually a full-time employee of the State or city governments and is relatively immune from the political musical-chairs that marks American life. He combines the functions of coroner and pathologist, performing the autopsies and subsequently deciding on the nature of the death. He works in close collaboration with the police, though he is by no means subservient to them. Upon his decision may rest the instigation of a criminal investigation, but he plays no part in the judicial process, apart from giving medical evidence. The prosecution is handed over to the district attorney or other law officer, the duties of the medical examiner being limited to determining the nature of the death and keeping statistical records.

The medical examiner usually has a building and staff provided by the authorities, and in a city of any size will have assistant pathologists, toxicologists and lay investigators who are the counterpart of the English coroner's officers.

Altogether, the system is most attractive, the only drawback as at present practised in America being that the autopsy rate is low compared with this country; this is not a fault of the system but of the policies and perhaps the finances of those who operate it.

THE CONTINENTAL SYSTEM

European countries, especially in the north, have a long tradition of forensic medicine, going back far earlier than Britain. This is evident in the well-developed and comprehensive system of death investigation which they possess.

Prominent are the Scandinavian countries, especially Denmark, which probably has the best service in the world.

The Latin countries are not so well served, but the Germanic and East European States, including the Soviet Union, have devoted space, staff and money to provide a well-run system of forensic institutes that puts the makeshift British system to shame. These institutes are run either by the universities or directly by the State, or a combination of both. There is no coroner or his equivalent and the pathologist in charge is the professor of the institute, who somewhat resembles a medical examiner. All investigations are carried out through the police force and the legal aspects are dealt with by a judge or public prosecutor. One disadvantage of the system in some countries is the large say which police have in the decision whether or not to hold an autopsy; often examination is external only. Obvious criminal cases are not affected by this, but marginal cases may be missed and the statistical returns of causes of natural death must suffer in accuracy. Even so, the well-ordered running of the institutes and the uniform coverage over the whole country are to be commended. There is a stable career structure to attract specialist pathologists; the standard of evidence available to the courts is good and the individual work-load of the pathologists is light by British standards, leaving more time for detail and research. Whereas departments of forensic medicine are declining in England (1969 seeing the retirement of the last professor outside London and the London 'chairs' due for downgrading before long), on the continent, almost every university town has its well-entrenched institute with its own professor.

THE SCOTTISH SYSTEM

No coroner exists in Scotland, as their legal system survived the Act of Union in the early eighteenth century. Instead, they have a law officer called a procurator fiscal, who is appointed in every county by the Lord Advocate. His duties range far beyond the investigation of sudden deaths, and he is responsible for initiating most criminal prosecutions. The enquiry into unusual deaths is held privately, there being no public inquest except in the case of traffic accidents. The main disadvantage of the Scottish system, as with American and Continental services, is the low autopsy rate. Again, this is not an inherent defect in the system, but of the practice of the officials who administer it.

OTHER COURTS OF LAW IN ENGLAND AND WALES

Though the forensic pathologist will visit a coroner's inquest more often than all the other courts combined, it is the criminal courts that will provide him with the sternest challenge to his knowledge and his ability as a witness.

Until 1968 the next commonest court for him to visit was the magistrate's court. Where a death was due to criminal action and another person was being accused of murder, manslaughter, infanticide or causing death by dangerous driving, the Director of Public Prosecutions would recommend that proceedings be commenced. The accused would then be brought before justices of the peace or a stipendiary magistrate. In this case, though the building and magistrates would be the same, the court would not be sitting as a 'Petty Sessions' (that is, a court concerned with minor offences), but as 'examining magistrates' who would see if there was a sufficiently strong case for the accused to be sent for trial to the next Assizes.

Until the Criminal Justice Act of 1967 came into force the following year, all witnesses had to attend and their evidence was gone through verbally, with opportunity for cross-examination by the defence lawyers. This might take days in a complicated case and the whole proceedings would be reported at length in the newspapers, so that w hen the case came to trial at Assizes, it would be virtually impossible to find a jury who had not read all about the case beforehand and they may have already biased impressions. In addition, all the witnesses had to go through the same evidence twice.

The recent change in the law allows the magistrates to make up their minds on the documentary evidence of all the witnesses' statements, without the witness actually being in court. This is conditional on the legal representatives of the accused giving permission; if they so wish, the old procedure may still be used. Also, the Press is forbidden to print details of the evidence, again unless the accused person's lawyers wish otherwise.

Now, these committal proceedings can be completed swiftly and without sensation; the witnesses are rarely called and the pathologist is spared at least one set of draughty corridors in which to wait for hours or even days!

The real test of endurance comes with the actual trial. The magistrates have no power to judge any crime associated with a death, and this is the task of the red-robed High Court judge at the Assize court.

The word 'assize' comes from the old Norman-French *assaiyez* — 'to sit' — and originated in early times when the king's court shifted about the countryside as he travelled, with strings of would-be litigants trailing after him trying to obtain justice. Eventually, the court was settled at Westminster, but regular excursions of judges went around the country towns in rotation. This has developed into the present 'circuit' system; there are seven circuits in England and Wales, together with permanent courts in London (the Central Criminal Court in Old Bailey) and Crown Courts at Manchester and Liverpool.

In contrast to the days of 'fire and brimstone' advocacy of fifty to 100 years ago, the proceedings in court are now very restrained and gentlemanly, especially where professional witnesses are concerned. Even so, the cut-and-thrust of the barristers (especially those cross-examining for the defence) is none the less arduous for a medical witness, in spite of its decorum.

As the bluster has gone from the court-room, so recent years have seen the abolition of the often violent partisan spirit with which some professional witnesses were formerly bedevilled.

A Home Office pathologist or any other pathologist who has performed an autopsy at the request of the coroner and police, is a 'prosecution witness', though this should make no difference to the nature of his testimony.

Even so, with the best intentions, it is difficult for a doctor or scientist, after weeks of work on a case, to submerge completely his convictions that he is right and the other side are wrong, especially when the 'others' are doing their best to make him look an imbecile, albeit in the most polite manner.

Nevertheless, the plain facts must be given in evidence, including those which weaken one's own interpretation; the oath says 'the truth, the *whole* truth and nothing but the truth', and the doctor must ungrudgingly admit the feasibility of any alternative explanation put to him by the defence counsel, if he cannot honestly deny it from his own knowledge and experience.

The defence is an easier position; they can go for any wreak point in the prosecution and worry it until a hole appears. They are under no obligation to volunteer any factors which weigh against their own case.

Medical evidence is commonly used by the defence these days. As soon as any suspect is arrested, he is entitled to legal representation and financial legal assistance if required. Armed with this, his lawyer may at once retain an independent forensic pathologist to advise them on their line of defence, and not infrequently he may conduct a second post-mortem examination. In fact, in a case of criminally-inflicted death the coroner cannot authorise cremation until the trial is over, in case the defence require access to the body. At the short opening of an inquest, the coroner usually asks the first pathologist and a senior detective, if there is any likelihood of the body being required further — sometimes, it is kept for weeks or even months in cold storage.

If burial has been allowed, even exhumation may be authorised, so that the defence expert witness may have the opportunity to examine the remains. Thus in Britain, no stone is left unturned to give every possible chance to the accused.

A Home Office pathologist cannot act as an adviser to the defence if another Home Office man has conducted the original autopsy, unless specific permission is granted by the Home Office. This is a fairly recent ruling and is a safeguard to avoid the possibly embarrassing and apparently paradoxical situation of two similar experts giving different opinions on the same facts. This paradox is more apparent than real and lies only in personal interpretations rather than on hard facts. For instance, if the prosecution pathologist describes a bullet wound of the head, the pathologist for the defence is hardly likely to say that it was not there! But if the body temperature on discovery was 30 degrees Centigrade, then it is a matter of opinion about the length of time each pathologist considers to have elapsed since death, as will be discussed in the chapter on this subject. It is for the jury to make up their minds who they are going to believe, though both medical witnesses are acting in perfectly impartial good faith.

In years gone by, such impartiality was not always evident; there were also far fewer pathologists available, so that the few great experts, whom the newspapers had made household words, were virtually able to steam-roller any adverse opinion by the sheer weight of their prestige.

Quite often, the defence pathologist does not give actual evidence in the witness-box, but merely advises the legal representatives on the medical aspects of the case. The 'papers' are sent to him beforehand (usually the depositions from the magistrate's court) together with a set of police photographs, which are always made freely available to the defence.

The doctor studies these and sends a written report to the solicitors of the accused, who pass them on to the counsel 'briefed' to appear in court. In a murder or manslaughter, these barristers will consist of a 'silk' — a Queen's Counsel — together with a junior. Some time before the trial at least one conference is held and quite often the pathologist attends this in order to assist in preparing a plan of campaign.

At the trial, the doctor may be asked to sit in court throughout the medical evidence. He listens carefully to all that is said, so that he can assist the defence counsel in challenging any medical discrepancies and in detecting any possible lines of defence. The doctor usually sits behind the barristers, and there may be quite a lot of whispering, note-passing and even a request for an adjournment if a 'thin patch' is detected in the prosecution evidence.

Prominent Q.C.s have an uncanny knack of 'instant understanding' in most medical matters. Sometimes it causes some chagrin in the hearts of medical men to watch an expert barrister assimilate in five minutes complicated facts that took the doctor years to understand! Not only that, but the next day, in another court, the same counsel may show equal expertise in some abstruse problem of civil engineering!

As far as the actual ordeal in court is concerned, the procedure is the same for both prosecution and defence witnesses, the only difference being the 'batting order' of barristers asking their questions. The pathologist will be called to the witness-box, often a varnished, pulpit-like structure in many of the older Assize courts. There he will be sworn by the judge's associate, a gentleman in a morning suit. The counsel will then enquire his name, address and qualifications to establish his expert status to the court. Following this, in the case of a prosecution witness, the counsel will lead the doctor through the whole of his post-mortem report and its interpretation, just as was done at the magistrate's court or, more usually these days, as given upon the depositions to that court. Following this, the prosecution may enlarge upon the conclusions and opinions of the doctor upon the facts just related.

The judge may ask additional questions at any stage, not only for his own edification but if he feels that some matter has not been explained fully enough for the lay jury to grasp. One of the marks of a good medical witness is the ability to put across medical facts to the jury in a comprehensible w ay — especially when they seem to be either deaf, asleep or supremely disinterested!

The newly-qualified doctor, especially at inquests and in minor cases at a magistrate's court, is often asked by a caustic coroner or stipendiary to speak in a language that everyone can understand.

The faults of immature pomposity are illustrated by the common classic of calling a black eye an 'acute peri-orbital haematoma'! Even though the coroner, magistrate or judge may know perfectly well what it means, the relatives and any jury present have a right to an intelligible description.

Returning to the court procedure, the prosecution counsel sits down when this 'examination-in-chief' is completed. The defence counsel then rises. As has already been said, the days of ranting, abusive barristers has gone, but well-mannered verbal dagger-thrusts can be just as destructive of a witness. The defence counsel will ask the doctor about any points in his evidence-in-chief that need clarification, then attempt to shake some or all of his opinions. As with disputes between pathologists themselves, it is rarely the hard facts that are argued over, but the interpretation of them. In an alleged strangulation, there may well be small haemorrhages in the skin of the victim; the defence counsel will hardly try to shake the doctor as to their actual existence — in these days of expert photographic records, this would be folly — but may very well try to shake the doctor's resolve in saying that they could only have arisen as a result of asphyxia due to strangulation. Armed with both his own knowledge from previous cases and the detailed ammunition supplied by the defence pathologist, the barrister may pursue the witness through all the alternative causes of such haemorrhages and attempt to shake his adherence to the original theory. This may be done directly, as a straight challenge to the knowledge and experience of the witness, especially when matched with text-book quotations of contrary opinions made by well-known experts, but often more devious paths are followed. Starting with some apparently innocent questions, defence counsel may work around to a verbal trap from which there may be no escape — the 'have-you-stopped-beating-your wife' gambit!

The experienced medical witness can see these coming and take steps to head them off. He will volunteer little to counsel, the volubility of a medical expert often being inversely proportional to his experience, as even a casual addition to an answer may be grasped by an astute lawyer and used to belabour the witness.

A fundamental difference is apparent in the training and perhaps philosophy of the lawyer and the doctor. In law, things tend to be 'black or white' with questions answerable with a yes or no. In medicine, as with all biological sciences, facts are of various shades of grey, rather than exact absolutes. Many times, the barrister tries to pin the doctor down to a straight 'yea' or 'nay' on a matter which cannot be so answered — then accuses him of evasiveness when he wishes to qualify any reply to the point of ambiguity. It has been laid down by a judicial decision that a medical witness may be allowed the opportunity to amplify his answer in the cause of justice and the Assize judge is there to see fair play if counsel presses too hard for an impossibly precise answer.

Even with the judge's welcome intervention, a strenuous cross-examination can be an exhausting affair. After a couple of hours in the witness-box, a doctor may emerge feeling as if he has just gone twenty rounds with Cassius Clay!

The cross-examination may be followed up with the 're-examination.' This, in the case of a prosecution witness, is carried out once more by counsel for the Crown and is intended to repair any damage to his case wrought by effective defence attacks. It is a rule that no new evidence may be touched upon, only clarification of what has gone before. If the doctor has had to retreat a little before the accused's counsel, the prosecution barrister may again repeat the salient points of that part of the examination-in-chief, in an attempt to plug any holes that may be obvious to the jury. If the case has been well prepared and the medical witness experienced, there may be very little, or even no re-examination.

No new evidence must be introduced, mainly because this is the last examination of the witness and the defence would have no opportunity of cross-examining again.

The pathologist, like any other witness, is liable to be recalled at any later stage in the trial, to clarify his evidence further, but in practice, the prosecution counsel makes an application to the judge for his release as soon as he has left the witness-box. If the defence agree, the judge invariably gives permission, and the doctor, breathing sighs of relief, hurries away, often straight to another court or to work which has been waiting for a day or more.

In a busy Assize, with more than one court in operation, the pathologist may even be shuttling between the two, with worried-looking policemen and court officials trying to avoid him being wanted in two witness-boxes simultaneously.

Even more common is the clashing of Assizes with coroner's inquests. In a busy city or district, inquests are daily affairs and a long murder trial may last a week or more, so the flitting to and fro becomes even more marked, especially if long distances are involved between the courts. In point of fact, the coroner's court has precedence over all the other courts — perhaps a survival from the time when the matter of the king's purse was more vital than justice — but it would be a brave witness who tells a Judge of Assize that he has to wait because he is needed first at a coroner's inquest!

The other courts that might involve the doctor are those of the civil side of the law.

The lower courts, like County Courts and Magistrate's when sitting on civil matters, rarely need medical evidence, but the various divisions of the High Court not infrequently need a doctor's expertise to help them reach a decision.

Though Admiralty is virtually immune from medical evidence, the other two parts of that division, namely Probate and Divorce, may call the doctor.

Probate has occasionally needed medical knowledge in settling disputes over wills where the mental state of the testator is in doubt — this so-called 'testamentary capacity' usually involves the family doctor or possibly a psychiatrist and certainly not a forensic pathologist, though the latter has to have a knowledge of the subject in order to instruct medical students, the future family doctors who may get involved with this rare, but highly contentious matter.

The divorce courts very often hear medical evidence of varying types. These will be mentioned in other parts of the book, but basically consist of evidence of adultery, either by scientific examination of clothing, the impossibility of parenthood as disclosed by blood-group tests, or the duration of pregnancy.

In the rarer cases of nullity of marriage, again medical evidence is of primary importance. In all these matters, serologists, gynaecologists and psychiatrists figure in place of the forensic pathologist.

The main platform for the pathologist is in the Queen's Bench Division, where a mixed bag of civil suits are heard. These take place at either the Royal Courts of Justice in the Strand or at the various Assizes before the judge hearing civil cases. Probably the most common kind of case is compensation for accidents, either industrial or traffic. Either employer or insurance company may resist a claim by relatives for compensation for some fatal mishap, which has already been heard at the coroner's court. Medical evidence may be the keystone of the case for or against the plaintiff.

The basic point of dispute over medical evidence in these cases is whether the alleged negligence of the defendant actually caused the death. Many cases involving road accidents have revolved around the contention of the defendant that the deceased was suffering from some disease like coronary thrombosis which precipitated the accident or even that the deceased was already dead when the vehicles collided. Here, only expert interpretation of the post-mortem findings can decide the issue; with many thousands of pounds at stake, these are often fought as hard as any criminal case.

Deaths due to industrial disease such as pneumoconiosis (dust-disease in miners and quarry-men) are less common now due to National Insurance schemes, but industrial accidents are very common sources of litigation. In non-fatal cases, surgeons and other specialists may give expert evidence as to the expected recovery or loss of function which will affect the victim's future earning power. In fatal cases, any dispute about the cause of death or contributory factors will require the interpretation of the pathologist, as in the road traffic cases.

In conclusion, it can be seen that the forensic pathologist's professional life is by no means confined to the sensational murder investigation. In some parts of the country he might go weeks or even months without seeing a homicide, but his use to the community in filtering off the natural from unnatural deaths, providing disease statistics of use to medical research and public health, investigating suicides, traffic, domestic and industrial accidents, assisting in civil suits and in teaching medical students and policemen, is far more useful to the community than a mere medical Sherlock Holmes, the usual and very inaccurate picture projected by the popular publicity media.

THREE — THE DOCTOR AT THE SCENE OF THE CRIME

Probably the best way to describe the procedure at the scene of a fatal crime or other suspicious death, is to create an imaginary incident and follow it through to illustrate the part played by the doctor. Though fictitious, the circumstances are unfortunately close enough to reality to be enacted in earnest somewhere in the British Isles every couple of weeks — and, in some countries, every couple of hours!

It is almost midnight in a large industrial city somewhere in Britain. In one of the less salubrious districts the public houses have been shut for some time. On this winter Saturday night the streets are empty apart from the occasional drunk or courting couple.

In a street of drab terraced houses the quiet is suddenly shattered by a piercing shriek and a young woman rushes out of a front door on to the pavement. She is over-dressed and over-made-up and has just returned from a rather poor night's business in the city centre.

The girl runs to the front door of the next house and hammers on the knocker, but before it is opened, several windows nearby light up and heads are poked out. A man and a woman come to the door and after some hysterical gabbling, they go into the house next door. The man rapidly comes out, several shades paler in the face, and runs for the phone box on the corner. Already half a dozen people have appeared — apparently from nowhere — and are converging on the house, where the two women are snivelling in the doorway.

Almost as soon as the next-door neighbour returns from the phone box, a blue and white 'Panda' car turns the corner and draws up at the house. The neighbour hurries up and directs the police officer into the house.

"In here, mate." He points to the front room, the first door off the dark passage.

The impassive constable treads heavily into the room, then stops dead just across the threshold — at first glance, it is all too evident that more than just a 'Panda-man' is needed.

In the untidy, cheaply furnished room, a young woman lies on the threadbare carpet. She has one foot still inside a built-in wardrobe and has obviously fallen out of it when the door was opened. Dressed in a garish dressing-gown, she lies very still. A trickle of pink fluid runs from the corner of her mouth on to the floor. Her face is very dark and although she seems dead, the experienced policeman still treads cautiously across the room and gingerly puts the back of his fingers against her forehead. It is warm, but not warm enough, and has the clammy feel of death.

He moves back, his part played out. The neighbour is standing close behind, goggle-eyed, but the officer waves him away. Pulling the door shut by fingernails gripping the panel edge, he shepherds the man and the two women to the front door-step.

"Who is she?" he asks firmly.

Through her sobs, the younger woman explains that it is her room-mate, Peggy. The officer, knowing his area well, is under no illusions as to Peggy's line of business, but that is no particular concern of his now.

"You found her?" he asks.

The other girl explains how she came home a few minutes ago, went to the wardrobe to hang up her coat and the other girl fell out at her feet. She was in normal health when she left her at six o'clock. No, she didn't know what Peggy was doing that evening.

The constable shunts the women back into the next-door house and leaves the shaken neighbour on duty at the front door. By now there are a dozen spectators, half in shabby dressing-gowns and raincoats over their pyjamas. Even the inevitable small boy has appeared, though it is now past midnight.

This is something with which the P.C. feels more at home.

"Right, clear off, sonny ... Back from the door, all of you. You may as well go home, there's nothing to see here."

The crowd shuffle back a token 6 inches, then obstinately stick. The officer turns his back on them and speaks into his tiny personal radio, which is clipped to the inside of his jacket. He notifies his own divisional station, who pass on the message to information room at headquarters.

Within three minutes, there is the noise of a 'hee-haw' siren approaching and a large black car slides around the corner, blue light flashing. Two motor-patrolmen jump out and go in for a quick look at the scene. By the time they emerge, another 'Panda' car has arrived, and the constables push the unwilling spectators further back.

One of the patrolmen is a sergeant and, after a word with the first constable, he goes into the next-door house, where the girl is sitting in a passage on a kitchen chair, drinking a double-gin and being comforted by the rather blowsy wife.

A few more minutes sees the arrival of a private car with the local detective-inspector and another 'Panda' car with a chief inspector from the uniformed branch of the division. These two inspect the death room briefly, then go across to talk to Maggie, the dead woman's companion.

After this, the senior officers and the sergeant put their heads together.

'Anyone told the Super yet?'

"I asked information room to do it," says the sergeant.

The divisional detective-inspector scratches his head. "May as well get on with calling the pathologist; tell information room we need a photo team and the Special Incident car; and the fingerprint boys."

"The police surgeon is on his way ... He was already in the station taking blood from a drunken driver," the uniformed chief inspector adds.

A few moments later, the detective chief superintendent arrives, having been caught by the phone just as he was going to bed. He is Mr. Harbuckle, the head of the Criminal Investigation Department for the city. He works from headquarters, but each division in the various parts of the city has its own C.I.D. under a divisional detective-inspector — the 'D.D.I.'

In serious crimes, which always include potentially criminal deaths, the headquarters will take over from the division.

Sometimes, the onus of calling the pathologist is reserved for the C.I.D. chief, but very often a working arrangement exists where the first relatively senior detective on the scene will do so, in order to save time, especially where the doctor has to come a long distance.

While the mobile sergeant is relaying these messages on his car radio, the chief superintendent is being brought rapidly up to date on events by the other officers.

He has a quick look at the scene, again without disturbing anything before the forensic experts come.

By the time he comes out, the police surgeon, Dr. Faust, has arrived.

The C.I.D. chief greets him informally. "Looks a straight 'up and down' murder, Doc ... We've got Dr. Crippen on the way, but you'd better have a look at her first."

The main purpose of the police surgeon's visit is to officially confirm the occurrence of death. Also, if the pathologist, Dr. Crippen cannot be found, or is delayed for a long time, the police surgeon might hazard an opinion on the time that has elapsed since death.

While Mr. Harbuckle goes to interview the other girl and the neighbours, Dr. Faust passes the sentry on the other front door and goes inside.

Already, another constable is standing inside with a clip-board, writing down the names of all who enter and leave, even senior detectives, so that any artefacts in the way of trace evidence or spurious fingerprints may be sorted out later.

The doctor crosses the room delicately, his hands in his pockets. He has thrown his cigarette away in the street and takes great care now not to add anything nor take away anything in the room, even such an insignificant thing as cigarette ash or a matchstick.

He stands near the body and looks at it carefully, noting the position, the carelessly arranged clothing, the colour of the face and the object around the neck.

He crouches down and gently feels the skin of the forehead, then of the hands, trying to gauge the temperature. Risking raising one of her eyelids, he studies the pupil and the white of the eye. Finally, just to make sure, he feels the pulse and cautiously listens to the chest with his stethoscope, putting the instrument on top of the dressing-gown in order not to disturb the clothing before photographs are taken.

This is about all he can achieve without interfering too much and he rises and creeps out just as cautiously.

Seeking out Mr. Harbuckle, he gives his brief opinion. "She's dead all right — a few hours, by the look of it, no more. Seems to have been strangled by that stocking around her neck."

Now the photography squad arrive in their van, closely followed by the fingerprint men.

The photographers set up their big tripods and Press cameras, and the house is soon erupting with brilliant electronic flashes as they take pictures of the scene from the front door, the room door and inside the room.

While they wait for the pathologist, they take as many photos as they can, but some will have to wait until the body is moved.

It is about an hour after the discovery of the crime that the forensic team arrive. Dr. Crippen arrives just ahead of the scientific officer on call for the Home Office laboratory, who is accompanied by another detective-inspector, the liaison officer from the 'lab'. His job is to act as an intermediary between the scientist and the police, advising on packaging and labelling of the exhibits.

The pathologist and the forensic scientist work very closely, as their functions are complementary and sometimes overlap. The latter's responsibility is to observe any non-medical aspects of the scene and to take any samples he thinks useful. Many of these are taken from the body by the doctor and handed over to the scientist; other things are dealt with entirely by the pathologist.

The two boffins go into the room and take in the general scene, which is all too familiar to them after some years at this work. Their experienced eyes will look at the general lay-out, the relationship of the body to the objects in the room, and bloodstains, tears or scratches on the walls, floor or furniture and any abnormalities on the clothing.

The pathologist kneels to look closely at the skin of the face and neck.

"Have you got all your photographs?" he asks Detective Chief Superintendent Harbuckle, who stands patiently behind them. The senior detective says he has, and the doctor then feels free to handle the body and move it about a little. The detectives tell the scientific experts the outline of the story as they know it. "Both of the girls have a poor reputation," says Harbuckle. "Not proper professionals, but at least part-timers."

The doctor nods over his task. He knows that murder is a well-known occupational hazard of prostitution. He looks at the congested face, the small haemorrhages in the eyelids and skin and mentally chalks up a diagnosis of asphyxia. There is a dark stocking wound around the neck, but he knows better than to touch it at this stage. Like the police surgeon, he feels the skin to gauge its temperature, but also flexes the elbows, neck and legs to test the degree of rigor mortis. Then from his black bag, he produces a long thin cardboard tube and slides out a thermometer.

This is not a doctor's clinical thermometer, but a long chemical one with a wide range of temperature reading. He places it in the armpit, through a convenient tear in the seam of the dressing-gown and closes the arm over it to wait for the mercury level to settle. When he has read it, he makes some mental calculations, his own brow wrinkling with the effort. "More than two hours, less than eight — may get a bit nearer later on, but I doubt if we can improve on that."

The detectives nod. "Doesn't matter about the eight hours, Doc," says Harbuckle. "We know she was seen alive at about six o'clock."

After another close look over the front of the body, aided by the scientist, who picks off some suspicious-looking hairs and flecks of thread (which he immediately puts into cellophane envelopes and hands back to the liaison officer to label), Dr. Crippen turns the body over gently and looks at the back and the floor underneath. While the body is held, more pictures are taken of the floor and the back of the body.

The scientific officer finds some more fibres and some bits of dried earth, which he delightedly puts into small plastic tubes and seals down.

"What about the ligature?" asks the detective-inspector from the division.

The pathologist gingerly tests the tightness of the stocking. "Safe enough — it will stay in place all right until we get her to the mortuary." He turns to Harbuckle. "That's all I can do here ... We can shift it as soon as you like."

A plain police van has already been called, equipped with a thin fibre-glass coffin, called a 'shell'.

Before being placed in this, the body is lifted gently on to a large new polythene sheet laid on the floor of the room, so that if any tiny bit of trace evidence — even an eyelash of the murderer — should fall off the body, it will not be lost, but caught in the sheet. Such a tiny fragment of evidence may be enough to help identify and eventually convict a suspect, if successfully matched with identical traces found in association with him.

The body, wrapped in its sheet, is placed in the shell; this is then taken straight away to the mortuary, which may be one belonging to the local authority, but more often it is one attached to a hospital.

As soon as the body has left, some of the photographers get busy again, taking the rest of the room from different angles, previously made difficult or impossible because of the body. They also take pictures of other rooms and access to this room, as well as the exterior of the house in some cases, having to return in daylight for this.

The forensic scientist also often returns next day for a really thorough search of the room; after the body has left, the room is sealed and a constable is left on guard all night to see that no one interferes with the possibly vital evidence still remaining.

The fingerprint men have done some of their work, though they, too, may want to come back and really go over the place with their brushes, powder and sprays. The more people that trample around during the investigation of the scene, the less the 'dabs' men like it, as then there are more spurious prints left behind to complicate their job. This is one reason why an officer is detailed to record all entrants to the premises, so that any strange fingerprints found can be eliminated by comparison with those of someone coming to the scene. At one murder, great trouble was experienced because one set of prints could not be matched — they were eventually traced to the assistant chief constable, who had popped in to see what was going on! Another, possibly apocryphal, tale is told of a police-surgeon who left his umbrella, complete with fingerprints, in the flat of a murdered prostitute!

The senior detectives usually go along to the mortuary, along with the forensic scientist and photographers. An assortment of other police officers are usually there as well, and frequently both the scene of crime and the mortuary look like a football crowd — a far cry from the usual detective novel where an inspector, a sergeant and a local bobby on a bicycle apparently are the sole participants in the investigation!

Important members of the team are the liaison officer and an 'exhibits officer' whose responsibility it is to collect every exhibit and see that it is labelled and listed with complete and utter accuracy. This has developed into a highly elaborate ritual, which tends to be the over-riding consideration at a crime scene, called the 'continuity of evidence'.

Every sample must be accounted for by some person who can be called as a witness in the subsequent trial, and it is better and more economical of manpower to designate one officer — usually a detective-constable or sergeant — to do this, rather than half a dozen policemen each with one or two objects to 'prove' in court.

The defence, especially if driven back to the wall with an otherwise hopeless case, might try to get vital evidence disallowed by challenging the prosecution to verify the authenticity of the 'clues'.

For example, if a strand of blond hair is found on the body of the dead woman in our fictitious case, the prosecution case may lean heavily on the fact that it matches exactly the hair of a blond man known to have been with the girl that night.

The defence may say that the hair is *not* the one that was found on the body at the post-mortem, and if there is a weak link in the 'continuity of evidence', the proof of identity may be ruled out by the judge and the prosecution case may fall flat on its face. They must be able to call the pathologist to say on oath that he found the hair and handed it to Detective-Constable Green, who can be called to say that he labelled it in a container (which is produced in court and handed to him to swear to) and took it to the laboratory, where he handed it to Dr. Black, the principal scientific officer. Dr. Black might even be called upon to say that he kept it under lock and key whilst in his care and that it was handed back to D.C. Green to bring to court as an exhibit. It is no good the pathologist saying that he thinks he put it on the top of a cupboard in the mortuary and a mortuary keeper kept it in a drawer until a porter took it across to Dr. Crippen's secretary, etc. etc. — unless all those people can be called and definitely swear on oath that they handed the sample along the chain of evidence without a blank spot anywhere.

The same procedure must be carried out in respect of the actual body of the dead woman. Someone who knew the woman in life must come and testify that the body was definitely that of Peggy So-and-so. At the mortuary, on the night of the post-mortem examination, someone must identify the body to the pathologist, so that there can be no possibility of error. This is done either directly by a relative, identifying in the presence of police officers, or a police officer who either knows the deceased from past experience or who has just had the body identified to him by a relative.

Any failure to keep each of the links of this chain of evidence intact may be seized upon by the defence and could ruin the whole prosecution case.

At the mortuary, the body is taken from the shell and laid on the autopsy table, still in its plastic sheeting. The clothing is then carefully removed, piece by piece, and wrapped in new brown paper. Polythene bags may be used, but only as a temporary cover, as damp or perspiration-stained clothes will rapidly become mouldy on storage. Each parcel is labelled and listed by the exhibits officer, before transit to the laboratory.

The scientific officer is satisfying himself at this stage that nothing is being lost from the clothing or body surface — if any loose hairs or foreign material is seen, he carefully collects it. When the body is lifted on to the table, he makes sure that nothing is left behind on the polythene sheet.

The old idea of the 'slab' is now outdated and the post-mortem examination is carried out either on a shaped porcelain table, or on a stainless steel trolley or table. Some are extremely elaborate and surpass operating theatre tables for their complexity. In fact, the whole of a really modern mortuary resembles an operating theatre, even to the elaborate multi-directional overhead lighting and the glistening cleanliness of the fabric and equipment. Unfortunately, these are still in the minority and, with the exception of a few mortuaries in large towns, the general standard of public mortuaries leaves very much to be desired. The mortuaries of hospitals are usually much better equipped and these are used for preference, though they are intended for the National Health Service and not the coroner and police.

With the body undressed upon the table, the pathologist makes a careful external examination and studies the back, limbs and orifices before going back to the most obvious place, the head and neck.

In this particular case, the stocking around the neck is of prime importance. It has been wound twice around the throat and tied in front. To preserve the knot, which may have some peculiarity in the method of tying which may be associated with some future suspect, it is not just untied, but cut cleanly through at the back or side, the loose ends sometimes being tied with twine to prevent unravelling. The cut ligature is carefully removed and placed in brown paper.

Dr. Crippen then looks at the underlying neck and is slightly surprised to see several prominent bruises as well as a deep groove from the tight stocking.

More photographs are taken while the doctor discusses this new development with the scientist and detectives. The significance of the extra bruises means that the girl was strangled manually before the stocking was put around the throat. This may have some influence on the tactics of counsel at any subsequent trial, but the job now is to examine and record every tiny facet of the physical appearances.

The body is measured for height and will later be weighed by the mortuary attendant, who has been roused from sleep and now hovers about with instruments and clothing for the pathologist.

Dr. Crippen, when gowned, aproned and gloved, carries on with a minute examination of all the signs of violence. These are either written down by a policeman at the doctor's dictation or are recorded direct on to a tape recorder, ready for transcription on to a typed form the next day. Some up-to-date mortuaries have a microphone fixed to the table or wall, which connects either with a recorder or direct to a secretary in another room.

The recording method has not yet met with ready approval by all Assize Court judges; in days gone by, the rough notes taken at the time had to be produced in court to 'prove' the authenticity of the tidy typewritten copies. If crumpled and blood-stained, this added to their air of genuineness, if not hygiene. In these modern days of tape or disc recording, the typewritten transcripts are the only 'originals' available and some august judges still grumble — and even some defence counsel, if all else fails them — but the practice is now so widespread that it becomes a case of 'take it or leave it'.

The autopsy goes on as the pathologist dictates his findings. The external appearances are usually even more important than the internal dissection in criminal cases, where external violence is the cause of death. Further specimens are taken for the forensic laboratory as the operation proceeds; the completeness of this sampling varies with the type of case, but head hair — with roots — eyebrows, blood and urine are almost always taken. In appropriate circumstances, pubic hair, moustache or beard hair are retained; in cases with a sexual or homosexual background, secretions from the orifices may be needed. The lips may be scraped for traces of lipsticks and the skin for cosmetics, as these may have left contact traces on the malefactor. Finger-nail scrapings, the finger-nail clippings or even the nails intact may be needed if there is any possibility that the dead woman tried to defend herself and may have shreds of the assailant's skin beneath them; these may be partly identified by blood-grouping, as will be described in another chapter.

Before any internal dissection, the temperature may be taken either in one of the body orifices or even through a small slit in the skin, as long as the latter does not interfere with the examination of injuries. This may give a slightly more accurate — or less inaccurate! — estimate of the time of death. The environmental temperature at the scene of the crime will have been taken and someone will have a record of the weather at the time, as this may have a bearing on the estimation of the time since death, especially in bodies discovered out of doors.

Once all the external examination and photography has been carried out, the internal dissection begins.

All organs and parts of the body are examined, whether directly involved in the injuries or not. Negative findings can be as important as the positive ones, especially where natural diseases may be alleged by the defence to have caused or contributed to death. A person with heart disease may not survive a battering that would not be fatal to a healthy person, and although this is usually no defence in law, it may have some effect on the sentence.

Also, the thoroughness of the examination might disarm the criticisms of a defence barrister seeking to discredit the worth of the pathologist as a witness, by exposing his failure to look at all the organs of the body. Though thankfully less common than in years past, one defence tactic, when the real merits of the case are hopeless, is to attack the competency of witnesses for the prosecution. Thus in a case of strangulation, the failure of the pathologist to notice a club-foot might be used as a weapon to show the jury that the opinion of this careless, inept doctor is worthless!

The examination completed, the pathologist carefully retains any material that might be needed for further examination. This is his responsibility, apart from blood grouping and analysis of body fluids for drugs and alcohol etc. Under the Coroner's Act, within which the pathologist is working (for in theory, at least, he is doing this examination for the coroner, not the police) he is entitled to retain any tissues and organs which he deems necessary for the proper determination of the cause of death. He could keep the whole body indefinitely, but in practice, small pieces of tissue are taken from every organ and wound, preserved in formaldehyde and later processed in the pathology laboratory for microscopic examination; this aids the doctor in the confirmation or exclusion of natural disease, the determination of whether wounds were caused before or after death and the age of the wounds.

Newer techniques have made these estimations of more value than they once were and this accentuates the need for fully trained, experienced men with knowledge of, and access to, the latest laboratory facilities.

In our imaginary strangulation, the windpipe, tongue and larynx ('Adam's apple' region) will be kept, especially for detailed dissection and microscopic examination, to see if certain small bones have been fractured, which may help to reconstruct the actions of the killer.

Another aspect exists to this retention of the relevant tissues. The defence have a right of access to the autopsy and any material retained from it. It is rare for the defence to send anyone to the actual post-mortem examination, because this is done at such an early stage that usually no charge has been made against any person and often even no suspect is available. In the rare cases where a person has been charged before the autopsy, then the defence lawyer can ask another medical man to attend the examination. More often, due to the usual delay, the pathologist retained by the defence has either to conduct a second autopsy or to content himself with an examination of the photographs, autopsy report and examination of the tissues kept by the first pathologist.

These items are not given into the charge of the exhibits officer and the pathologist is responsible for their safe-keeping and maintaining the 'chain of evidence'.

The photographs taken at the scene of the death and at the post-mortem are made into large prints by the police photography department and bound into cardboard albums. A number of these albums — sometimes dozens in an important case — are prepared so that copies can be given to the pathologist, the defence, the prosecution counsel, the jury and judge. The photographer who took them has to come to the trial — or his deposition read out in these more sensible days — to 'prove' that he took them and that the 'unretouched negatives are still in his possession'.

The whole post-mortem examination may take many hours from start to finish, depending on the complexity of the case. Much time is spent in waiting for photographs to be taken and the elaborate continuity of evidence procedures to be performed, such as identifying the body and all the samples which are to be exhibits in the case. Other frequent delays are the difficulties in transporting the body to the mortuary, lack of a mortuary assistant and several other hold-ups that are almost inevitable, especially if the scene is in some remote rural locality.

In cases such as shooting and the 'battered baby' condition even longer delays may be encountered, due to the need for X-ray facilities. Most criminal cases seem to be discovered in the late evening, especially on Friday and Saturday — this is associated with British drinking habits — so the remainder of the night is spent at the scene and in the mortuary. Add a round trip of 150 or more miles driving and the ruination of many a forensic pathologist's week-end is easily explained!

The location of a murder makes a considerable difference to the basic routine of our hypothetical case.

Bodies are frequently concealed in remote places in the countryside, especially in woods. The examination of these scenes may be very difficult, compared with indoor urban crimes. All forensic pathologists have memories of ploughed fields, dense undergrowth, treacherous quarries, thick woods and desolate moorlands, often swept by biting winds, driving rain or snow, all usually in pitch darkness!

Many police forces now have special equipment to deal with such scenes. 'Special Incident vehicles' — either vans or large estate cars — carry all manner of devices to preserve the integrity of the scene no matter what the weather. A large polythene tent on a metal frame — the size of a garage — can be erected over a body within minutes to protect it from rain or snow. Large flood-lights on tripods, powered by either bottled gas, car batteries or a portable generator, can illuminate a night scene; lately, very small petrol generators, able to be carried by hand, have become available.

Some police forces have large trailer caravans fitted out as mobile headquarters; fitted with radio and carrying high telescopic aerial masts, they are used as an operations room at the actual scene of crime, in touch 'over the air' with the distant information room at headquarters.

At least one force has a mobile canteen which can feed the large investigation team during the many hours or even days that a scene needs to be examined.

From the forensic pathologist's point of view, it is no good trying to perform an autopsy in any but the best available conditions. The state of many rural and small urban mortuaries — as well as some in great cities — is appalling, and most of the work has to be done in the National Health Service facilities of hospitals. Nothing is to be gained by attempting an examination with grossly inadequate space and equipment, even if available near the scene of the crime, so sometimes the body has to be taken many miles to a satisfactory mortuary.

At the conclusion of the post-mortem examination, the pathologist will discuss his findings with the senior detectives. He gives not only the bare medical facts, but explains their significance and interprets them in the light of his experience, to reconstruct as much as is possible of the actual crime.

In our fanciful case, it was apparent that the woman had been strangled manually first of all, then the stocking tied around as an afterthought, probably when she was already dead. The distribution of marks on the neck indicated an attack from the front and the pattern made it tempting to suggest that a right hand had been used — but the pathologist was too wary to commit himself definitely on that.

The time of death was not very important in this case, as the woman was known to have been alive six hours before being found — the pathologist and the police surgeon agreed in saying that their estimate of the time since death was more than two hours and less than about eight.

With a woman who was virtually a prostitute, no opinion could be given on the probability of recent sexual intercourse — there was certainly no evidence of a forcible sexual assault. There was no natural disease that could have caused, accelerated or contributed to death, which was asphyxia due to strangulation.

By this time, it is approaching four o'clock in the morning and the pathologist goes wearily home for a few hours' sleep, being thankful that at least it is now Sunday and he will not have to cope at nine o'clock with a full day's routine at the university.

The police disperse about their various tasks — the senior detectives will have no sleep this night, having to see as many witnesses as possible and arrange for the next series of enquiries to be made.

They have already heard from neighbours that there was a frequent male visitor to the house, and when they have as accurate a description as they can ferret out from the witnesses they circulate it to all divisions, adjacent police forces, their own criminal records office in the police district and to Scotland Yard, who hold a national records system. An 'Identikit' picture is often built up from recollections of the more reliable witnesses and this is circulated to newspapers and television companies in certain cases.

The Chief Constable will have been informed of the murder, as with all serious occurrences and he will no doubt discuss with the detective chief superintendent the advisability of asking for the assistance of Scotland Yard. Here the crime fiction writers are much nearer the mark when they portray the reluctance of many detectives to 'call in the Yard'. This is especially so in recent years with the widespread amalgamation of police forces into large units. The original idea of the Metropolitan Police supplying assistance was due to their greater experience in dealing with major crimes, usually murder, compared with the numerous small forces who rarely had occasion to be involved in criminal death investigation.

Now that most of the provincial forces have become so large — and also have the regional crime squads as a reserve force — much of the need for assistance has gone, except in very complicated cases or where the ramifications spread over a large area of the country into different police regions. When the assistance of the Yard is required, it is the usual practice, after a consultation between the Chief Constable and the head of the C.I.D., for London to be contacted by telephone. There is a rota of a senior detective superintendent and a sergeant on call for such requests and they can be on their way within hours of the crime being discovered; they may be away from the Yard for an indefinite period, stretching sometimes into months as in the Cannock Chase investigations. This assistance is free if requested within twenty-four hours of the discovery of the crime, otherwise the local police authority has to pay the expenses of the Yard men.

In cases of complicated murders, where the identity of the criminal is not obvious (this is the exception, as the majority of homicides occur within the family in Britain), a well-established routine is set up by the police. This often includes a 'murder-room', which is a temporary headquarters near the scene of the crime. It may be in a police-station, but can be in part of a school or any other convenient building commandeered for the purpose. As already mentioned, in rural surroundings some police forces have a mobile office.

A phone system is installed, if not already available, and a military-style 'operations room' is set up to co-ordinate all the activities in this urgent business. Trestle tables, telephones, masses of paper and endless cups of tea are the impressions left by a visit to a murder room in full swing. There is usually an officer at the door recording arrivals on a clip-board, and members of the public who have any information to give are directed to appropriate officers to tell their story. In a really obscure murder, there may be massive house-to-house searches and interviews with all the men in a town, for example — which runs into thousands of items to be recorded. To avoid the one vital clue in all this deluge being overlooked, a rigid and precise method of sifting information must be used, and formerly it was the experience of Scotland Yard officers in this sort of work that made them so useful.

This does not directly concern the forensic pathologist, except that he may be called more than once to the operations room to give an opinion on some new feature or to elaborate on a finding at the autopsy. Sometimes a weapon is found in the course of the big search and the detectives wish to know if it could be connected with the crime. The doctor may be asked to look at it and give his opinion on whether or not it can be discarded.

Again, when a suspect is found, the doctor may be asked to examine him for injuries caused during the struggle etc. Though this is usually done by the police surgeon, where the latter has attended the scene previously, the pathologist may be asked to examine the suspect, thus avoiding calling two medical men to a lengthy trial. Usually, a blood sample is needed from the suspect, to be sent to the forensic laboratory for matching against any stains found at the scene or on the body. The pathologist may take this, again in order to avoid involving another doctor in the 'continuity of evidence'.

Examination of the suspect may be of great assistance if trace evidence is found at the scene. Blood stains, the clothing, cuts and bruises, pattern of the soles of shoes etc. have all helped to convict murderers in the past, and this aspect will be described in more detail in other parts of the book.

To return to our fictitious homicide, let us imagine that two days after the discovery of the body, the mysterious boy-friend of the dead girl is detained by the police, so that he might 'help them with their enquiries'!

He strongly denies having been near the house that night, but cannot produce any satisfactory alibi. The police will invite him to make a statement and may ask him if he will allow them to examine him and his clothing. He may refuse, but if the police feel that they have a strong enough case, he might be charged with the murder, when he will have no option but to submit to examination. The clothing will be sent to the Home Office laboratory, both that which he is wearing and any that they suspect he might have been wearing on the evening of the crime. The man himself will be examined either by Dr. Faust, the police surgeon, or by Dr. Crippen.

Let us say that the accused, John White, has a scratch down his left cheek. His clothing shows slight bloodstaining on the left lapel of the jacket, but the blood tests reveal that this is of the same group, A, as his own, not the girl's, who has a different group, Group O. Thus the stains are likely to have come from the injury on his own face.

But the front of the girl's dressing-gown also had a dried bloodstain — and this was Group A, not her own. This is suspicious, but by no means proof of anything, as some 40 per cent of the population have this group. Other tests narrow this down to a much greater degree of correspondence, but at the present state of scientific knowledge, it can never be said that a given stain came from a given person. If the group had *not* been Group A, then the stains could definitely *not* have come from the man; thus blood group evidence can only be *exclusory*, never confirmatory.

Though it seems a little too good to be true, let us also suppose that the fingernail scrapings so carefully preserved by the pathologist at the post-mortem, reveal tiny shreds of skin when examined at the laboratory. These can be grouped in the same way as blood and turn out to be Group A, the same as John White. It is also possible, in favourable circumstances, to tell the sex of the skin from microscopic examination of the cell nuclei — this is not absolutely fool-proof, but the suggestion here is that the skin was male. None of these facts are cast-iron proof of identity by any means, but they all help to add bricks to the pile of circumstantial evidence which will be put before the jury.

Though it would be like the answer to a forensic scientist's prayer, let us also suppose that a hair picked from the dressing-gown of the girl exactly matched one of John White's in colour and physical characteristics and that a flake of earth retrieved from the floor matched exactly the clay in his garden 25 miles away. These illustrate the need for preserving every scrap of evidence at the scene of crime, which otherwise might be lost for ever if not rescued in the early stages of the investigation.

Within a few days of the murder the coroner will hold a short preliminary inquest — the so-called 'opening', at which a relative will formally identify the dead girl. The pathologist will give the bare cause of death — 'asphyxia due to manual strangulation' — but there will be no elaboration of the medical evidence at this stage, as controversial points must not be discussed in public before the case comes to trial.

Chief Superintendent Harbuckle or one of his senior detectives will tell the coroner that a person has been charged with murder; the coroner will then adjourn the inquest under Section 20 of the Coroner's (Amendment) Act, either indefinitely or for a token period of two or three months. If the pathologist and the senior detective both assure him that they know of no reason why the body may not be disposed of, he will issue a burial certificate to the relatives so that the funeral can proceed. If it is known that the defence require a second opinion, this may be delayed until the other autopsy can be carried out, unless this has already been done.

In any event, no order for cremation can be granted, as this would naturally destroy any further evidence available by exhumation. If cremation is insisted upon by the relatives, it must be delayed until after the result of the trial at Assizes.

After the trial is over, the Clerk of Assize will notify the coroner of the result and usually the inquest is never resumed, whether the accused be found guilty or not.

If no person is charged with causing the death within a reasonable time — usually a few months — then the coroner must hold a full inquest with a jury to ascertain "where, when and by what means" the deceased came to his death. The inevitable verdict is "murder by person or persons unknown" in an obvious case of homicide. The inquest in these cases seems rather futile, as it is a bit much to expect a jury of nine or ten lay citizens to arrive at a better result in half an hour than a whole police force could after months of intensive investigation!

During the weeks after the arrest of John White, the police are active in finishing the collection of all their evidence and in preparing it for the scrutiny of the Director of Public Prosecutions. All serious offences in England and Wales are submitted to his department (which is situated in the Old Bailey) for an expert legal opinion as whether or not to proceed with a prosecution. Naturally, in a case such as ours, this is virtually inevitable, but borderline cases may be rejected where the evidence is poor and there are other considerations which would make a prosecution hardly worth undertaking. This most frequently happens in infanticide, dangerous driving causing death and similar conditions. As an instance, a recent case concerned two infanticides discovered forty years later, admitted to by a now elderly woman; the D.P.P. quite understandably advised that no action should be taken.

In the usual type of murder, the Director will supply a solicitor from his own department to handle the case right through and this representative will attend both committal and trial proceedings.

Now that committal at Magistrates' Courts usually consists only of a production of documents, the first court the pathologist will attend will be the actual trial itself. This may be several months later, especially if the murder was committed in the early summer; by the time the case is ready for court, the last Assizes may have finished and the case will have to wait until October.

In the meantime, the defence is active, and John White's solicitors will have briefed a Q.C. — often called a 'silk' from the type of gown he is entitled to wear. The solicitors will have worked up the case and retained an independent pathologist, if they feel that he can contribute anything to the defence. This procedure has been described already, the pathologist either examining the documents, photographs and material kept by the prosecution doctor or he may even have performed another autopsy himself. Similarly, they might also engage a non-medical scientist to advise them on possible loopholes in the evidence of the hair and soil which is helping to damn John White.

Non-medical scientific matters may be of great importance in certain cases — one only has to think of the 'mummy' murder from North Wales a few years ago, where many hours were spent at the trial in arguing textile technology in connection with the stretching properties of fabric that was found around the neck of the deceased.

At the trial, the procedure will be as described in the chapter on the role of the doctor in death investigation. Dr. Crippen will give his evidence, be cross-examined and no doubt re-examined. In such an impossibly loaded case against the accused, there would almost certainly be a plea of guilty, if the defence could make out some extenuating circumstances that would reduce the charge to one of manslaughter. If White said that the girl tried to rob him, or taunt him or otherwise provoke him, then this might add weight to his story that he grabbed her in temper around the throat, but with no intent to kill. The fact that death was a pure asphyxial one, rather than a sudden death due to pressure on the large blood-vessels, somewhat tells against this story, as it means that the gripping must have taken some time; these are the points that will be hammered out in the witness-box. The prosecution will try to make the most of this long time factor, whilst the defence will do all they can to refute it.

The stocking around the neck is another bad jolt for the defence, but they might have precedents for explaining it away.

In a very similar murder in the North Country, a man strangled a prostitute because he discovered her going through his pockets with intent to steal. There was a folded chair-cover bound around the neck, though she had been strangled manually; the accused explained this, by saying that he thought the ligature would obliterate his fingerprints on the skin

In a straightforward case like ours, the pathologist will have little to disturb him in the witness-box, but in many of the other cases quoted in this book, both doctors and scientists have finished their evidence exhausted or shaken — or both!

But here, the long night's work at the scene of the crime will undoubtedly have led to a conviction, and John White will leave the

Assize court to do the few years of his 'life' imprisonment at least in part due to the efforts of a doctor and a scientist.

FOUR — PROBLEMS AT THE SCENE: (i) TIME OF DEATH

Two major questions arise almost immediately at the scene of every criminal or suspicious death — who was the deceased and when did he die?

Very often the answers are so obvious that even to ask these questions seems puerile. Yet on occasions the obvious has been far removed from the truth. A body found in a house is naturally assumed to be a resident of the premises, though this is not always so. In most instances there will be ready witnesses to the identity of the victim, if not to the actual commission of the crime.

Most difficulties in identification arise when the death is discovered either after a long delay or when the body is found away from the home, especially hidden out-of-doors. In fact, much of the technical expertise needed to identify a corpse is necessary because of long delay after death and it will be better to look at the 'when did he die' problem before returning to methods of identification.

The determination of the time of death has been a perennial problem in forensic medicine for many years; in spite of numerous attempts to improve accuracy, little progress has been made and the estimation still consists of a mixture of science, black magic and inspired guesswork!

The more experienced a forensic pathologist becomes, the less willing he is to be tied down to an accurate estimate; in fact, the exactness of a doctor's pronouncement in this context is often in inverse ratio to his experience. What an expert pathologist *can* do with confidence, is to offer to the detective officers a *range* of times within which he feels sure that death occurred. This is a much more valid method, though often disappointing to a police officer who is trying to crack the alibi of his prime suspect.

Certainly, the picture drawn in detective novels, films and television of a doctor confidently saving "Yes, he's been dead two hours and a quarter" or "He must have died last Tuesday week" are calculated to send a pathologist into hysterics of either laughter or rage! After the passage of forty-eight hours, one is lucky to get the right *day* of death, and as time goes by, even the week, month or year becomes sheer guesswork.

This focuses attention at once to a very significant aspect of calculating the time of death — as the moment of death gets more and more remote in time, so the error in estimation increases. Yet even very near the point of death, the errors are great; though the *absolute* error may be less, the *percentage* error may be as bad or even worse. For example, a man may be shot dead at midnight and is seen by a doctor at two a.m., when the time of death is estimated as having been one hour previously. In another case, a man shot dead at midnight may not be discovered until midday, when the time of death was estimated as four a.m. Though in the first case the doctor was only an hour out, he was 50 per cent in error, whilst in the second case he was wrong by four hours, yet was only 33 per cent in error.

In spite of this, the general rule holds good that after the first day, the accuracy — if such a term can be applied to the ritual — falls off very sharply, and from the point of view of alibi and general confusion of the circumstances, it is certainly true that the longer a murderer can keep the body of his victim concealed, the more chance he has of getting away with the crime, other factors being equal (which they rarely are!).

Coming to more specific details of how the time of death is estimated, we must briefly see what changes occur in the body after death. The actual definition of the moment of death is controversial, but for our purposes here, we can take death to mean the cessation of the heart beat. As soon as this stops, all other vital processes begin to decline. They decline at different rates according to the complexity of their functions. The brain stops working within seconds and becomes irreversibly damaged in a few minutes. Skin, hair and nails take a long time to 'die', though the hallowed legend of corpses growing beards and long hair in the coffin is nonsense. Other organs have an intermediate reaction to stoppage of the heart, but all gradually stop their metabolic processes of converting nutriments into energy and thus stop producing *heat*.

This is the most important factor in calculating the time of death and is the one on which virtually all methods of estimation depend.

The normal body temperature is 37 °C (98.4 °F), and shortly after death, this begins to decline. Unfortunately, the rate of fall does not follow the regular pattern seen in the physics laboratory. With the complex shape and constitution of a human body, the theoretical colling curves are greatly distorted and this rules out the use of accurate formulae for calculating the rate of heat loss.

The first inaccuracy is seen in the initial hour or two, when instead of a steady decline of temperature, there is a level plateau of variable size, due to both poor conduction of heat from the exterior and the residual metabolic activity of various tissues, which survive for some little time after the heart stops.

The next part of the cooling curve is the most useful for the forensic pathologist. Armed with his long thermometer, he takes the temperature in a body orifice or inside the actual tissues. At the same time, he measures the environmental temperature at the scene of the death.

A basic calculation is made, the actual mathematics depending on the particular doctor's training, experience or prejudice! Many research workers over the years have produced formulae for estimating the time since death — in fact, probably more papers have been published in scientific journals about timing of death than on any other single forensic medical topic.

The calculated answer is no more than the crudest mid-point of a possible range of times, and anyone attempting to use the actual numerical value as more than a very approximate guide is suffering from a serious delusion.

The basic calculation may be made in several ways; probably the least inaccurate method is to multiply the fall from normal in degrees Centigrade by a factor dependent on the environmental temperature. For example, if a body is discovered with a temperature of 27 °C, then this constitutes a *fall* of 10 °C from the normal of 37 °C. The figure 10 is multiplied by 1 ½ if the environmental temperature is 15 °C giving a time of 15 hours since death. If the temperature at the scene was 0°C, then the factor is only 1, giving a time of 10 hours, and so on for other local temperature conditions. Another rule of thumb is to assume that a body loses 1 ½ °F each hour.

Yet this is only a start. The basic figure must be modified by yet another crude rule-of-thumb to take into account the following causes of error.

Firstly, correction must be made for the amount of clothing or other covering on the body. It is obvious that a nude body, especially in outdoor conditions; will cool far faster than one wrapped in an overcoat or one found in bed under blankets and eiderdown. The victims of murder are not infrequently hidden and the concealing materials, such as sacks, straw etc., may be a very significant addition to ordinary clothing already on the body.

Secondly, the physique of the dead person is important. The rate of cooling is dependent on the ratio of weight to body surface area. Children and thin persons have a larger weight: area ratio than fat people. Also, the presence of a thick layer of fat under the skin in corpulent people again retards heat loss, as it acts as an efficient insulator.

Thirdly, the posture of a corpse makes an appreciable difference. A body crouched in a corner, with the back against a wall, the arms and thighs pulled down against the trunk, will cool much more slowly than one spreadeagled with all surfaces exposed.

The fourth factor is very important and very obvious — this is that the environmental temperature alone is not a measure of the true conditions. A current of moving air has a far greater cooling effect than still air at the same temperature. The presence of water or even merely damp conditions will also hasten cooling. Not only this, but one can rarely be sure that the environment has remained the same ever since death took place. A body left in the open on a sunny afternoon may not be discovered until night, when there may even have been a frost. A corpse in a cold room may have been lying in front of a coal fire eight hours previously. In the open, weather conditions, rain, wind strength etc., may all vary enormously.

The last, although this is by no means an inclusive list of errors, is the fact that we so far have assumed that the body temperature was 37 °C (98.4 °F) at death — but this is frequently not so! A person dying of a fever or of a certain kind of cerebral haemorrhage or head injury may have a temperature of 106 °F. Conversely, as deaths in very cold conditions may show as much as 10-20 °F drop at the time of death; after severe blood loss from some knife wound or other injury there may also be a lowered temperature at the time of death. Both these conditions will throw the calculations way out.

In the sadistic sex-murders of the Heath' case (1946), one victim was found naked in a hotel room, her body temperature at 6.30 p.m. being 84 °F (29 °C). From circumstances, it was known that she had been strangled somewhere near the preceding midnight, yet assuming her temperature was normal at the time of death, this would indicate that she had cooled less than 15 °F in eighteen hours, though unclothed. One explanation of the discrepancy was that her temperature was *not* normal at the time of death; the congestive episode of asphyxia has been known to produce a rapid rise in temperature.

From all these sources of error, any of a score of permutations can be made which will make a complete nonsense of any attempt at accuracy in estimating the time of death. Even the most experienced forensic pathologist will be defeated when he tries accurately to calculate the hour of death in a fat man spreadeagled naked in a field where a howling east wind has arisen a few hours before.

All that can be done is to offer to the investigating officers a time bracket, the width of which varies according to the number of imponderables present.

Once the temperature of the corpse has reached its lowest point, little information can be gained. The temperature never gets to that of the immediate environment, except in freezing conditions, as bacterial action, similar to that in hay-stacks and compost heaps, maintains some heat and actually causes the body temperature to rise a few days after death, due to frank decomposition.

In average conditions, the minimum temperature is reached soon after the end of the first day following death, so the usefulness of body temperature as a guide to time of death is confined to the first twenty to thirty hours.

Many other methods of estimating the death period have been attempted, including several biochemical analyses of body fluids, but they all suffer from the same disadvantage that all chemical processes in the body are extremely dependent on temperature changes. All the extraneous factors listed above wreak the same havoc with these techniques. Analysis of chemical constituents of the blood, the cerebro-spinal fluid and especially the fluid of the eye have been tried, with little practical benefit. The fluid from the eyeball was used because it is in a remote site, relatively free from post-mortem changes and early bacterial action. The levels of potassium, Vitamin C and other biochemical substances have been investigated, but appear to offer no advantage over the straightforward temperature method; they have the added disadvantage that they require complicated laboratory facilities and a lot of time. The detectives want to know the facts at the actual scene and the pathologist, equipped with only his thermometer, can supply just as accurate information in the present state of our knowledge.

When the temperature has dropped to near-environmental, there is little but general observation, experience, further guesswork and intuition to guide the pathologist.

In past years, much reliance was laid on rigor mortis as a useful guide to time of death, but this has fallen into disrepute. Rigor mortis is a generalised stiffening of the muscles which occurs after death, due to accumulation of acid products of metabolism which turn the proteins of the muscle into a rigid substance.

The speed of this chemical change is very variable, and again, temperature changes modify it considerably. In the 'average' body dying in a normal house temperature, a very rough approximation can be made by saying that rigor mortis takes twelve hours to develop fully, lasts another twelve hours and then gradually fades over the next twelve to twenty-four hours. The stiffening of the muscles does not occur all over the body at once: the small muscles, such as those of the eyelids and jaws are often the first to be noticeably rigid in about three to six hours. The process then spreads to the arms and legs, being complete at anything up to a whole day after death.

The rigor passes off in about two days in the same order as it appeared. This relaxation is due to the onset of putrefactive changes and early dissolution of the body tissues by the action of enzymes. Once gone, it can never return, as the chemical structure of the muscle proteins has been irreversibly altered.

Many factors alter the appearance of rigor mortis — in fact, it sometimes may never appear at all or be so weak as to be almost undetectable. Violent exercise shortly before death may greatly hasten the onset of rigor, because a large quantity of acid substances are manufactured due to the active energy production of the muscles. These are then readily available to convert the proteins into the rigid compounds.

Conversely, a weak, emaciated person dying slowly after a debilitating illness may show almost no stiffening.

Death in very cold conditions, such as freezing outdoor temperatures, may completely inhibit rigor mortis until the body is taken indoors, when the cycle will start. This obviously ruins any attempts at using rigor as a measure of time of death. A spurious type of rigor may occur in extreme cold, due to virtual freezing of the body fluids, but this vanishes on moving to a normal environment, to be followed later by true rigor, as already mentioned.

At the opposite end of the temperature scale, burning or extreme overheating of a body may cause rapid stiffening due to heat coagulation of the muscle proteins — here, no true rigor can ever occur.

Between these extremes, moderate warmth or coldness hasten or delay the onset of true rigor, again emphasising the temperature dependence of most post-mortem changes and thence their unreliability as an indicator of time of death.

A curiosity associated with the subject of rigor mortis is the rare condition of 'cadaveric spasm' which has developed almost into a forensic legend. This is an instantaneous rigor coming on at the instant of death, usually in only one part of the body, such as the hands, though sometimes it is generalised. This peculiar state is invariably associated with a violent death or at least intense physical or emotional activity. Most cases in civil practice have been seen in drowning, though it has been recorded on battlefields since time immemorial.

The mechanism of instantaneous cadaveric spasm is quite obscure. The typical findings are of tightly clenched fists immediately after death, long before normal rigor mortis could have occurred. Objects are often grasped in the hands; in drowning, grass or weeds are clenched in the fingers, indicating a desperate attempt at salvation in the last seconds of life.

Of more direct forensic significance, suicides have been found immediately after death with a pistol immovably grasped in the fist, at once confirming the impossibility of murder, as this rare condition cannot be simulated. A pistol pressed into the hand of a shot person might be held rigidly after some hours due to normal rigor mortis, thus simulating suicide, but cadaveric spasm cannot be so engineered.

Similarly, great medico-legal importance must be attached to the rare cases where a murdered person grasps a button or hairs etc. from his assailant and retains it in a spasmodic grip until discovered at autopsy. The more frequent occurrence of instantaneous cadaveric spasm under conditions of war is well known and must in some way be related to the heightened tensions of fear, emotion and exercise associated with the battle.

Continuing along the time scale after death, we have seen that temperature estimations are the most useful during the first day or so, then the presence of rigor or its absence may be of some slight use in the second or third day.

After this, things go from bad to worse for the pathologist, in relation to guessing the time of death.

The next stage is somewhat objectionable and concerns the dissolution of the body. Bacteria from the intestines rapidly spread throughout the abdomen and then to other cavities, followed by percolation along blood vessels to other parts of the body. Once again, temperature is the great mediating influence and no strict timetable can be drawn up. We can say roughly that the first discoloration of decomposition begins about the third day and is well advanced over the whole body by a week.

Many factors other than temperature modify this, to the chagrin of the doctor. Persons dying of a heart condition where there is much fluid in the body — formerly called 'dropsy' — tend to decompose much more rapidly. The opposite is true for people dying with dehydration, possibly from some emaciating condition or after dysentery. This is possibly one explanation for the frequently-noted good preservation of victims of arsenic poisoning; there may be some direct effect from the germicidal properties of the arsenic, but probably the severe loss of body fluid during the sickness before death is of more relevance.

The usual progression of post-mortem 'autolysis', as it is scientifically named, may be grossly distorted by environment. Sometimes dead persons die alone in a small room heated by a gas or electric fire. If not discovered even for only a day or two, autolysis may be greatly accelerated; the same may apply if an electric blanket is in use.

The opposite condition is obvious — cold may completely retard all decomposition, as in the Siberian mammoth discovered in 1901 when some of its meat was fresh enough to be eaten after 10,000 years! The principle is universally applied in mortuaries, where bodies awaiting examination and burial are stored in huge refrigerators at a few degrees above freezing. If prolonged storage is required (as in the current American fad for attempted immortality) then deep freezing to — 20 °C or even — 70°C will completely suspend all traces of dissolution for an indefinite period.

From the practical point of view, the pathologist can only relate the appearances to his previous experience, making mental allowances for factors like environment, and come to some necessarily wide range of times during which he considers that death must have occurred. He can be wildly wrong, especially when dissolution of the body is advanced and all he has to work on is a heap of bones, with or without some repulsive soft tissues.

Before going on to the consideration of these skeletons, mention must be made of special cases where the body is recovered from either water or soil.

Using death in normal air conditions as a standard, then an approximate rule-of-thumb states that decomposition under water is only half as rapid and burial in the ground is only an eighth as fast.

Naturally, as in all medical and biological matters, these generalisations are so crude as to be almost useless (a fact which is often hard to get through to the precise minds of lawyers in court). The type of water is very important, besides its temperature. Decay of a body in sewage-contaminated effluent of an industrial river will be far faster than in the clear water of some mountain stream. Bodies recovered from water after a few weeks' immersion frequently show gross changes which make identification difficult. The skin of the hands may peel off like a glove, rendering fingerprinting difficult or impossible. Enormous swelling of the features and body renders viewing by relatives distressing and usually valueless. The hair may be lost and the eyes clouded so that many of the usual identifying criteria are absent.

Burial in soil, either as a means of criminal concealment or respectably in a coffin, raises its own problems. The regular cemetery burial will present no difficulties in identification or time of death, as these will have been recorded, but the concealment of homicide by burial raises special problems.

Unless discovered soon after death, the buried corpse without a coffin decomposes at a rate which varies according to climate, depth of interment, the nature of the soil and its moisture content. Though slower than on the surface, decay is still rapid and after a few weeks, identification may be impossible. Added to this is the problem of accelerated decay by insects. In actual fact, the action of animal predators, both great and small, is far more important in bodies on the surface or in water, than deep in the soil. In sea water, both fish and crustaceans can wreak great damage on bodies in a short time. On land, especially in wooded and lonely rural areas, large animals such as foxes add their activities to those of the ubiquitous insects whose natural function it is to clean the face of the earth of dead fauna, which includes humans.

Two unusual processes must be mentioned here, as they have had profound medico-legal implications on certain occasions. Though the usual progression of decay goes through liquefaction of soft tissues to the eventual production of a dry skeleton, at extremes of dryness and dampness this can be modified into two different processes which preserve the body. The first is well known — that of 'mummification'. Both the ancient Egyptians and other people have used this as a means of preserving the body; the Egyptians used a combination of embalming and climatic drying to achieve their ends, but some South American tribes used merely to leave the intact corpse to their hot dry climate to produce a shrivelled but recognisable permanent mummy.

Under certain conditions, mummification can occur in Britain, where an artificial environment is suitable.

By far the commonest type of mummy is the concealed, new-born baby. Many times each year, dried baby bodies are discovered in attics, drawers or suitcases where they may have been concealed for many years without decomposition. A newly-born child is almost sterile as far as bacteria are concerned and so the decomposition-making germs from the gut are absent. The child, whether stillborn or the victim of infanticide, may be concealed in a place conducive to mummification. Dehydration, perhaps aided by a warm current of air then takes place. Suitable sites are lofts, perhaps against a warm chimney-breast or a drawer in a warm room. Often the only further decomposition that occurs for many years is attack by mice or moths.

The converse of mummification is that peculiar change which may occur in damp conditions, called 'adipocere'. The normal body fats, especially those which lie under the skin, consist of neutral fats which are liquid at body temperatures. After death, if ample water is present, a very slow chemical change often occurs. The neutral fat is 'hydrolysed' into a mixture of fatty acids and soaps, producing a solid white greasy or waxy substance which is very stable and may last unchanged for many years. The change may take place in drowned bodies within a few weeks, but usually takes longer. Though commonly seen in fragments of many exhumed bodies, sometimes it is so widespread as to preserve the shape and features of a corpse well enough for visual recognition after many years.

Neither of these special post-mortem changes is of much use in helping with the time of death, though naturally a *minimum* period of weeks or months may safely be assumed.

The last aspect of attempts to estimate the time of death concerns the examination of skeletons and bones, and in this context it is often impossible even to hit the right *century*, though the correct *millennium* is often attainable, except in the most remote archaeological specimens!

The estimation of date of skeleton material represents the borderland between forensic pathology, archaeology and anthropology.

Bones are very often discovered in these days of extensive rebuilding and ground clearance, and the forensic pathologist is asked for an opinion in cases where they have not come from some known archaeological site.

The first question he has to answer is the probable date of burial, which is usually approximately the same as the date of death. This apparently straightforward request is fraught with difficulty and once more the dogmatism of the answer may be inversely proportional to the experience of the examiner.

From the medico-legal point of view, the most useful test is to try to decide upon which side of a 'time threshold' the bones fall. This threshold is usually fixed at seventy to 100 years, as if the remains are older than this, then even if a definite homicide had occurred, it is almost impossible for the culprit to be brought to justice, as he will already be dead himself. Once this decision is made, there will be no question of a criminal investigation and usually the coroner will not want to waste public money by pursuing the matter any further. If the remains are thought to be more recent than, say, fifty years, then at least some enquiry is justified, mainly to try to determine the identity of the skeleton. Without any knowledge of the name of the deceased, again any formal enquiry becomes sterile.

The practical aspects of making this decision about which side of the threshold to place the bones, is far from easy. A body left in the open, buried in the ground or hidden in some secret place such as cave or cellar, will have undergone dissolution at a rate which varies widely. However, within a few years — unless adipocere or mummification takes place — all the soft tissue will vanish and bare bones will remain. Some tags of fibrous tissue, tendons and ligaments — the 'gristle' — may survive for a year or two in the open and much longer when buried, but eventually a skeleton is left. Once this stage is reached, further changes depend greatly on the environment and once more, the biological variations that so annoy lawyers, prevent any adherence to a time-scale.

Bones in dry, sandy soil may last in perfect condition for thousands of years — the Egyptian desert is a prime example, but, even in damp Britain, bones of pre-Roman people have been found in very good condition after burial in sand-dunes. Conversely, bodies interred in wet graves where frequent flooding occurs may vanish, bones and all, with a few decades, especially if the percolating water has come from peaty soils with an acidic nature. This attacks the calcium of the bones and reduces them to nothing in a few years.

All intermediate stages are possible and thus the appearances of bones must be related to the environment when being examined by the pathologist. It is true that in average conditions, a bone less than say, fifty years old, will be hard and firm to the touch and not crumbling at the edges. The density will be fairly high, due to the survival of the protein matrix which binds together the calcium salts which form the mineral part of the bone. As time goes on, the organic proteins decay and the calcium becomes leached out by water which is often slightly acid due to dissolved carbon dioxide. The proportion of protein remaining is one of the best indicators of age, even though it is still partly environment-dependent. A fresh bone contains about 5 per cent of nitrogenous matter, mainly in the form of protein. This undergoes little reduction during the first fifty to seventy years, the period of medico-legal interest. A bone with more than 3-5 per cent nitrogen is probably less than 100 years old, and having only 2 per cent or 1 per cent definitely excludes it from the interest of the law enforcement authorities and relegates it to the realm of the antiquarian.

Protein consists of a mixture of amino-acids, much simpler compounds also containing nitrogen. Fresh bone contains up to fifteen different amino-acids, including two special ones, the prolines. These can be analysed by a special technique called chromatography, and the total number counted. If the number found is more than seven, then the bone must be fairly recent, almost certainly less than 100 years; if the prolines are absent, then the bone is probably more than fifty years old.

Another test is the presence or absence of fluorescence when the cut surface of the bone is viewed with an ultra-violet lamp. A fresh bone will shine a bluish-grey in a dark room under U.V. light. As it gets older, the outer rim will progressively fail to fluoresce and eventually the whole thickness of the bone will remain dull under the U.V. lamp. Apart from a negligible surface crust, almost all bones under 100 years old will fluoresce right through; complete loss means great age, some fluorescence surviving in bones of even Norman origin.

Other tests such as the reaction to immunological sera, the persistence of a positive test for blood, the ultra-sonic conductivity and various staining reactions all have their place, but the results are very crude and often contradictory. A bone may be estimated as a certain age by one test and twice or ten times as much by another! Little accuracy can be hoped for, but usually a decision can be made about this primary allocation into the potentially forensic or the definitely archaeological.

Though not directly a medico-legal issue, it is an interesting paradox that the very much older bones can be dated with far more accuracy than the recent ones. This technique has almost revolutionised archaeology and is applicable not only to bones, but to wood, hair or any organic material and depends on the presence of carbon in the specimen — a substance invariably present in all matter of organic origin.

The technique is known as 'radio-carbon' or 'G14' dating and was developed by Professor Libby of Chicago in the late 1940s. The method depends on the fact that all living tissues take up carbon from the atmosphere during life, but naturally, not after death. Plants absorb atmospheric carbon directly as carbon dioxide during photosynthesis; animals take it indirectly by eating the plants or eating other animals who feed on plants. In any event, all our body carbon has ultimately been derived from the atmospheric carbon; most atoms of this carbon have the normal twelve electrons in each atom (C12), but due to the action of cosmic rays from outer space, some nitrogen (N14) in the upper atmosphere becomes converted to an unstable radio-active type of carbon (C14). The ratio of C14 to C12 has been constant for millions of years at 1:1,000,000,000. So during life, all plants and animals have a thousand-millionth part of their body carbon in the form of C14.

As soon as death occurs, assimilation of new carbon ceases. At the same time the unstable radio-active C14 begins to disintegrate at a constant rate, utterly independent of environmental or any other factors. Its 'half-life' is 5,570 years, so that 5,570 years after death, the C14: C12 ratio will now be only 1: 2,000 million. This process goes on unremittingly and at any point on the time scale, an estimation of the amount of C14 remaining will give a reliable measure of the time since death. The analysis is a highly complex and delicate operation, depending on the measurement of radio-activity of a known quantity of bone or other substance over a period of many hours or even days.

The big drawback from the forensic aspect is that the difference in the carbon ratio is too small to be measured in bones less than a few hundred years old, so that the age group that interests the pathologist is excluded from the method. At the other end of the scale, it can measure bones up to 70,000 years old, and a recent modification has extended this period even further into antiquity. For the archaeologist and palaeontologist the radio-carbon method is a gift from heaven; its use helped to date the Dead Sea Scrolls and to unmask the Piltdown hoax, where a scientist with a perverted sense of humour misled anthropologists for years with an ape jawbone that was alleged to be a form of primitive man. The C14 test finally confirmed the suspicions of some scientists that this bone could not possibly be as old as it was supposed to be.

Incidentally, the radio-carbon test has been ruined for further generations of archaeologists, as the pollution of the atmosphere since 1945 with atomic bombs has added great quantities of manmade C14 to the atmosphere, thus disturbing the ratio that has existed for aeons of time. However, another possibility arises in that the pollution of the atmosphere with all sorts of other radio-isotopes, such as calcium and strontium, will in future form a pattern when laid down in bone which might lead to a type of 'fingerprint' that can date a bone to a very short period of time. For instance, if a forensic pathologist of the year 2070 is brought a skeleton, radio-analysis may reveal a pattern of isotopes known to have been present in the atmosphere in the decade 1960-70. This will be of considerable use, providing that the amount of radio-active compounds in the environment have not made man an extinct species by 2070.

FIVE — PROBLEMS AT THE SCENE: (ii) WHO WAS THE VICTIM?

Though prosecutions for murder have been successful even in the absence of a body — the "Porthole case" and the Muriel McKay murder, for example — it is extremely difficult to obtain a conviction in a homicide, where the body cannot be identified.

An exception was the Rouse case of 1930. Rouse's Morris car was found burning one Guy Fawkes night near Northampton with an incinerated corpse lying across the front seats. It was taken to be Rouse at first, but it later transpired that he had picked up some unknown traveller and killed him with a mallet blow to the head. The body was soaked with petrol and ignited. The presence of carbon monoxide and soot in the body indicated that death had occurred after the fire began. Rouse's motive in wishing to be thought dead was an increasing burdensome number of adulterous affairs all over the country, around which he travelled as a salesman. He is strongly suspected of murdering a girl some months before the fire, but was convicted and executed for the killing of the man, the identity of whom is unknown to this day.

The problem of identification is bound up closely with the post-mortem changes described in the last chapter, except where death is very recent indeed. Once decay has set in — and especially when only a skeleton remains, then the techniques of discovering who the person was, become more complicated.

*

This is illustrated by the 'Mamie Stewart' case discovered in South Wales in 1961.

Some youthful 'potholers' entered an old mine-working on the cliffs near Brandy Cove, Caswell Bay, and discovered some human bones. When reassembled, it proved to be the dismembered skeleton of a woman, sawn into three sections through the upper arms and spine and through the thighs. The bones were clean and dry and appeared quite old. Remnants of clothing, hair, shoes and jewellery sifted from the cave rubble were dated in various ways and pointed to about 1920 as the time of origin.

Police records and old witnesses and newspapers were searched and the disappearance of a young actress named Mamie Stewart recalled in 1919. She had lived nearby as the mistress of an engineer, who later was imprisoned for bigamy. This man was sought again in 1961 by the police, who hoped he 'might help them in their enquiries', and was soon found — in a Bristol cemetery, here he had been buried in 1958 after dying from natural causes, almost forty years after committing the murder of which a coroner's jury found him guilty three years after his death.

In this case, all the usual methods of direct and individual bone measurement were made; the technique of photographic superimposition employed in the Ruxton and Baptist Cellar cases was also used with acceptable correlation.

With a perfectly fresh corpse, the methods of identification are more a matter of common sense and police routine, rather than science. The vast majority of sudden deaths are naturally identified straight away by relatives or friends. The man who is killed in a street accident is often first identified by the contents of his wallet, examined by a policeman or mortuary attendant (though a formal identification by a relative is almost invariable at a later date).

The next more difficult stage is that of someone found dead in lonely surroundings, even though it be just a hotel room, flat or lodging house. Again, personal effects are the usual rapid way of finding his name and permanent address, if he has one, but some vagrants or those on the run from the law may remain unidentified for days or even weeks. Here the machinery of police records is invoked; fingerprints are sent to the Regional Criminal Records Office and to Scotland Yard. If any previous conviction exists, the identity can be discovered in hours. 'Missing persons' lists can be checked, though this is by no means the comprehensive service that many people believe it to be — to go missing is no offence and the records the police keep are far from complete, depending only on notifications from the public on a local basis. In fact, probably the best missing person service is purely voluntary, that run by the Salvation Army.

Naturally, where a dead body is concerned — and urgently so if the death appeared homicidal — all possible means of identification are used. Photographs, suitably touched up to look lifelike, are issued to police stations, newspapers, television and perhaps by the hundred to detectives who go around the streets 'on the knocker', interviewing whole populations.

With a recently deceased person, such efforts are almost always successful before many days go by, though occasionally a complete blank is drawn, especially in London and other great cities. These unidentified bodies are often foreigners, with no relatives, records or local attachments to help the authorities discover who they are. Very rarely, a wrong identification is made; a body from the Thames was once declared at an inquest to be that of a certain mid-European woman. Unfortunately, the woman named turned up some time later, puzzled to find that she was officially dead.

The pathologist has little to do in these cases apart from providing the police with height, colour of hair and eyes (often a difficult thing to decide in the dead), the general build, details of teeth and any particular physical characteristics such as deformities, tattoos, old injuries or surgical operation marks, all of which might help relatives or acquaintances to recognise the description.

The real forensic medical functions come into their own when conventional identification is impossible, due to post-mortem decomposition, mutilation from injury, dismemberment or the action of fire.

The medico-legal problems involved can be amongst the most lengthy and laborious, but at the same time the most fascinating which the pathologist is ever engaged in. Many of the classical murder cases in British courts have included superb scientific evidence of identity — names like Ruxton, Christie, Crippen, Haigh and many others were national sensations at the time and are part of the forensic medical history of the country.

An account of the various techniques used is best divided according to the different parts of the great question — *whose is this body?* The answer to this ultimate problem is the sum of Sex, Age, Height and Personal Features.

SEX

The ease with which the sex of a body can be determined naturally varies greatly with the condition of the corpse and the amount of it available. In passing, it might be mentioned that the sexing of even a *live* human can sometimes be difficult to the point of impossibility, but although intersex problems have a forensic aspect, they are outside the scope of this book.

In the great majority of dead bodies, the determination of sex is obvious even with a severe degree of post-mortem decomposition. The external genitals, the breasts and the distribution of pubic hair usually offer an instant answer, and even when dissolution is very advanced, examination of the internal sex organs usually settles the problem. In fact, of all the organs of the body, the female womb is the most resistant to decay, being a hard, very compact muscle mass. Thus normal anatomical examination will clear up this question in all intact bodies which have not reached the stage of skeletalisation. A problem arises when gross mutilation has taken place and only parts of the body with no obvious sexual differences are available. This may come about from deliberate mutilation by a murderer, as in the Ruxton case, or from accidental injuries after death. These last are common in bodies recovered from the water, where ship's propellers and the contact with underwater obstacles may cause grievous damage. On one occasion, a foot inside a shoe was recovered from the edge of the Thames. From the size and style, it was obviously male, but no owner was ever discovered. It could not even become the subject of a coroner's inquest, as there was no proof that the rest of the body was not still alive — if it had been a *head*, it would have been a different matter! Other types of post-mortem dismemberment may occur in the countryside, where large predatory animals may drag parts of the body away. In a recent case in the West Country, the pathologist and police officers had to search an area of woodland to recover limbs of a man who had died almost a year previously.

Where only part of the body is recovered, sexing is a stage more difficult. All sorts of factors must be taken into account, depending on the part recovered and the state it is in. With fresh samples, the presence of make-up, nail varnish, amount and length of hair and bleaching or coloration of hair might suggest a woman, though of recent years even this has assumed less diagnostic value!

One of the classics of identification in British criminal annals is that of the Ruxton case in 1935. Ruxton was a doctor practising in Lancaster and was arrested on a charge of murdering both his wife and housemaid. Two weeks after they vanished, numerous portions of human body (eighty-six in all) were found scattered about a small valley in southern Scotland. They were in an advanced state of decomposition, but could be seen to belong to two separate individuals. The bodies had been dismembered in a way which suggested some knowledge of anatomy; they had been mutilated so as to make recognition, even of sex, as difficult as possible. Large pieces of both were never recovered.

Painstaking reassembly showed that both belonged to women, one about 5 feet 4 ½ inches and 36-45 years of age, the other 5 feet in height and 18-22 years old, both of which were consistent with the missing women.

Photographs of the skulls were compatible with photographs taken during life of the dead women. The hyoid bone of the older woman was fractured and there were other signs of strangulation, while the maid's body revealed a fractured skull. Some of the wrappings around the remains were traced to the doctor's house, and pieces of human flesh were found in the house drains. Bloodstains were found in the bathroom and on his suit. Ruxton was found guilty of murder and hanged.

A specific test for female tissue has been developed of recent years, which unfortunately is only applicable to fresh tissues. In 1949, two scientists, Barr and Bertram, noticed that the nuclei of most female cells contain a nodule, roughly the shape of a tennis racquet, which has since become known as the 'Barr body'. These are present in all cells, but are most easily seen in the white blood cells, the lining of the mouth and the skin. They are associated with the difference in chromosome make-up of males and females and a count of a sufficient number of cells will give a definite indication of the true sex. In fact, the use of the Barr body count is greatest in the cases of doubtful sex during life, but has on occasions been used to good effect in forensic pathology.

Where the remains are so fragmentary or so decayed that only bones are available for study, the subtle anatomical differences between male and female are called into use.

If the whole skeleton, the pelvis or the skull is present, then sex can be determined with virtually 100 per cent accuracy. Where big limb bones like the thigh are available, the chances of sexing the remains are also very high. If only small, isolated or fragmented bones are left, then the prospects are correspondingly reduced, though an expert anatomist can work wonders.

In these cases, the forensic pathologist, though he will form his own opinions, normally calls in the more expert advice of his colleagues in the anatomy department of his medical school. Here lies another justification for forensic pathology being concentrated in full-time university appointments, as it greatly facilitates access to the other experts like anatomists, odontologists, toxicologists, serologists and even more exotic specialists.

The more subtle sex differences of small bones may be only apparent to an anatomist, but the variations in larger structures are more obvious. The female pelvis is by far the most striking, as it is naturally related to the passage of the child during birth. The whole pelvic girdle is flatter and wider than that of the male. The 'pubic angle', the junction of the two halves between the thighs, is much greater in the female, being about a right angle. Many other minor differences exist and the ridges for muscle attachment are less prominent than in the male.

The skull is usually smaller than the male, as are all the bones, but there is such a wide variation that this alone is a poor criterion.

The eye sockets tend to be rounded in the woman and rectangular in the male, who also has more craggy eyebrow ridges and a more prominent jaw. The mastoid prominences behind the ears are larger in the male, but perhaps the most obvious feature is the general 'ruggedness' where larger muscles are fixed to the bone; this applies to the rest of the skeleton, too.

Definite sexing often depends on precise measurement of angles, lengths, widths and ratios of measurements, all of which needs expert knowledge, special instruments and availability of reference tables. Of recent years, the influx of large numbers of immigrants of varied ethnic groups has greatly complicated this work; there is a definite variation between even Celtic and Anglo-Saxon residents of Britain, so one can well imagine the differences seen in Asian and African races, especially when the race is quite unknown to the examiner of a heap of bones.

HEIGHT

After sexing comes an estimation of stature. Again the determination of height depends on the amount of body available and its condition. When the intact corpse is recovered, direct measurement gives an accurate post-mortem stature, but this may differ by an inch or more either way from the height recorded during life. This may be due both to slight lengthening or shortening after death and also due to the probably less accurate measurement during life.

When a dismembered body is concerned, the reassembly of the fragments and subsequent direct measurement gives an approximate answer, but should be checked by calculations from other bones, as described below. The same applies to an intact skeleton, which can be measured overall, then about an inch-and-a-half added to allow for the soft tissues of feet and scalp.

In the common circumstance of an incomplete skeleton, or even a single bone being found, the accuracy of height estimation depends on the type and number of bones found. If they are merely small bones of the hands or feet, spinal vertebrae or ribs, then very little help can be expected, but long bones from the limbs can be extremely useful in calculating the total body structure. Again, this is a job for an experienced anatomist, who will have a special measuring device called an osteometric board, as well as the very necessary experience.

Over the years, anatomists have drawn up tables of statistics based on the length of various bones in humans of known heights. These tables can be used to calculate in the opposite direction, that is, to find the height from a known bone length. Allowances have to be made for sex and age and also for race, where that is known. The thigh-bone (femur) is the most useful for this investigation, followed by the upper arm (humerus) and the lower bones of arm and leg.

Where the whole skeleton is present, marked disparities between total height and height calculated from various bones may lead an expert anatomist or anthropologist to suspect and perhaps identify the presence of an unexpected racial element — for example, the leg bones of a negro are much longer in proportion to the total height than in a European.

AGE

The third part of the question of identity concerns the age of the deceased and this can be very much more difficult than the previous two estimations. It becomes progressively more difficult with advancing age of the person; when a baby delivered before the full term of nine months is concerned, the age can be calculated with an accuracy of weeks. In childhood and adolescence, the age can often be predicted to the nearest year or so, but after the early twenties, the accuracy falls off sadly and by middle age it is frequently impossible to guess even the correct decade.

Leaving the matter of premature and newborn babies for the moment, the estimation of age of children and young adults depends largely on the changes in bones during the growing process. A child grows in height mainly by adding new bone at certain fixed growing points at the ends of his long bones such as the femur and humerus. While these growth centres, called epiphyses, are active, they consist of cartilage (gristle) instead of the dense mineralised bone of the adult. The epiphyses eventually begin to calcify and so become visible on X-ray films and later still they join up or 'fuse' with the main shaft of the bone at reliably constant times during the first twenty-five years of life.

By direct examination at autopsy or, much better, by X-ray examination, the doctor can tell if various epiphyses have or have not calcified or fused and by reference to anatomical and X-ray data, can estimate the age to within very close limits. For example, the knob at the top of the thigh-bone (the 'head' of the femur) calcifies during the first year after birth and fuses with the shaft between 18 and 20 years. One of the bones at the elbow calcifies at 11 and fuses at about 17. As this adolescent period advances, the dates become less definite; the last bones to fuse are parts of the hip, usually during the twenty-fourth or twenty-fifth years.

Girls tend to mature slightly faster, and frequently their epiphyseal dates are a year or so earlier than the boys. Similarly, the maturation dates in the tropics may be up to three years earlier in the later growth period.

Once all the bones have fused in the third decade, things become much more difficult for the forensic pathologist and anatomist. One of the few useful features after this time is the state of the skull. The vault of the cranium is made up of a number of flat bones which interlock at their edges by a fine serrated margin like the teeth of a saw or the outline of jigsaw pieces. In infancy, there are large gaps between them, filled only by fibrous tissue called fontanelles, easily felt on a baby's head. The one on the front of the head closes at about eighteen months.

Returning to mature adult life, these seams between the skull bones begin to fuse in later life, first on the inner surface, then on the outer, so that the irregular line vanishes. If none are so fused, then the skeleton probably belongs to a person of under thirty. Those in certain positions near the temple tend to join at about fifty, but there may be a variation of twenty years in the fusion. The whole method is unreliable but is sometimes the only straw that can be clutched.

At an even later time of life, the pathologist may only be able to say that the person was senile, though senility overtakes individuals at widely differing times. Signs of senility in the skeleton are increasing porosity of the bones, thinning of the jaws after loss of teeth, widespread fusion of the skull sutures and diseases associated with senility such as osteo-arthritis of the joints, especially the spine.

Beyond middle age, where soft tissues are present, then the cartilages of the voice-box become calcified and brittle, the ribs and breast-bone may show increasing calcification and the margin of the coloured iris of the eye may develop a characteristic cloudy ring, the so-called 'arcus senilis'.

Degenerative pathological conditions may give some clues, as in the detection of osteo-arthritis mentioned above. Extensive hardening of the arteries may exclude the remains from an early age group.

A father and son were lost at sea whilst fishing off the north-east coast. Some time later, a body was washed ashore, wearing fisherman's clothes which were identified as belonging to the son, a man in his twenties, the father being about 60. The body was too badly damaged for visual recognition, but on the strength of the evidence on the clothing, an inquest was commenced. At this stage, doubts arose and the inquest was adjourned whilst the body was examined by a forensic pathologist. It was soon apparent that the body could not possibly be that of a young man, as the skull sutures were fused, there was shrinkage of the jaw s where teeth had long been lost, the spine showed arthritis and the blood-vessels contained calcified arterio-sclerosis. All this was strongly indicative of an older man and burial under the wrong name was avoided.

One part of the skeleton is of major importance in the determination of age — the teeth. They are the most resistant parts of the whole body, and in the younger age groups can give very accurate information about age. Two sets of teeth appear, the milk teeth and the permanent teeth. Though there is a degree of variation, the dates of appearance of these are usually accurate to within a couple of years, especially in the child. The twenty milk teeth begin to appear about six months of age and are all through by about the end of the second year or slightly later. They begin to be shed when the thirty-two permanent teeth start erupting through the gums; the main set appear about the sixth or seventh year and all but the last four are in place by the age of 13. These four exceptions are the 'wisdom' teeth and they have the most variable time of appearance, usually between 17 to 21, though they can be a few years later.

The presence or absence of the various teeth can be a very exact chronometer up to the twentieth year, and together with the evidence from the epiphyses, makes ageng the body of a younger person a reasonably accurate exercise.

All forensic aspects of teeth are a specialist job for a dentist with special interest in this topic. An experienced forensic odontologist can deduce many other useful bits of information from the teeth, as will be described later. Still concerning ourselves with age, there are certain subtle changes due to wear and advancing years, which can help in arriving at the age of a body even in later life, when the evidence is all the more welcome. Even sexing can be assisted by dental examination.

A special mention must be made of the problems of determination of age in immature babies, that is, the foetus in the time between conception and full term, nine months later. This facet of ageing human remains is important, not least because of the frequency with which the problem arises. Dead babies are discovered almost daily in Britain, some being the victims of infanticide or abortion, others being stillborn. It is so easy to dispose of a newborn baby in secret and all sorts of hiding places are used to afford temporary concealment. Many are merely left in the open countryside, being dumped from cars. Others are hidden in public toilets, left-luggage offices, refuse tips and a hundred-and-one similar places where there is usually little hope of ever finding the mother. As mentioned under post-mortem changes, others may be hidden at home, either in attics, in chimneys or tucked away in drawers.

The legal aspects are discussed in the chapter about children but here a few points will be mentioned about the special problems of ageing the foetus and newborn child.

The developing individual begins as a microscopic egg and passes through a rapid growth phase, first being called an embryo, then a foetus. At the end of the full term of nine months, the baby is usually 18 to 24 inches long and weighs from 6 to 9 pounds, though it is common knowledge that the normal range can be very great. Other pointers to full term are the finger-nails, which then extend beyond the fingertips; the hair is at least an inch long; and the testicles are usually apparent in male children. Internally, a calcified growth centre is present in the lower end of the thigh-bone and in a certain ankle-bone.

Other estimates of age can be calculated from the length of the foetus. A rule-of-thumb hallowed by time is that the length in centimetres equals the square of the number of months of the age. It is important to be able to determine whether a foetus is more or less than twenty-eight weeks since conception, as this is the legal age of viability. Here again, bone centres are important, as well as length, weight and various features such as the eyes being capable of opening and the finger-nails nearing the finger-tips. In important cases, where a serious criminal charge may lie, the advice of either an embryologist or an obstetrician may be of great assistance to the pathologist.

Once the height, age and sex are settled, then attention is directed to any personal attributes that will help to put a name to the body, rather than just to assign it to one huge section of the population characterised by "a man 5 feet 9 inches in height, aged about 20".

Very often, these first characteristics of sex, size and age will be obvious, even with marked post-mortem changes which make visual identification impossible. Then the pathologist and the investigators will be immediately interested in any personal features; conversely if only a skeleton is available, then no further information may ever be forthcoming, apart from the teeth.

It is in the intermediate condition of post-mortem decomposition or mutilation that painstaking medical and dental work may bring useful results.

Obvious things like hair and eye colour have already been mentioned. Added to them are racial colour, tribal markings etc., in appropriate circumstances.

A woman's body was found after being murdered, with hair of different colours firmly clutched in each hand. A man named Ellison was later found to have gone to a barber next day, to have his hair and beard trimmed, the barber noticing that both had recently been hacked about by someone unaccustomed to hair-cutting. The hair was brown and the beard grey and matched those found in the clutch of the dead woman. Ellison was convicted of murder.

Skin and hair may resist putrefaction for many centuries, if dried in the early stages. This is illustrated by the examination in recent years of skin and hair which had been nailed for many centuries to the doors of Worcester Cathedral and other churches. Microscopy shows them to be definitely human, confirming the tradition of nailing the skin of those who committed sacrilege to the fabric of the churches they robbed.

Tattoos can be of considerable use as well as interest, all types are to be seen, from the religious to the obscene. Rarely is the name of the deceased present, unfortunately, though initials can be helpful. Tattooing used to be an indication of the social class of person, being common in seamen, soldiers and labourers, but since the last war, it has become so common (especially amongst young men on National Service) that this no longer holds good. A tattooed woman still risks the label of a prostitute, though again exceptions are numerous.

The pigment of a tattoo is deep in the skin and the shedding of the superficial layers in decomposed bodies does not affect its recognition. Particular types of tattoo have some recognition value — that of the concentration camp inmates is well known. Less well known is the fact that a bluebird design on the base of the thumb was a recognition mark between homosexuals, though again this has been swamped by people unaware of its significance. More recently, a certain symbol tattooed on the inside of the lower lip has been used by 'hard' drug peddlers as a recognition sign.

Though tattoos fade with time, the only way of removing them is by surgical excision or cauterisation, which inevitably leaves a scar; this in itself may be of forensic significance.

In the famous controversy about the heir to the Tichbourne estate, the missing baronet was well known to have been heavily tattooed on the forearms. An imposter named Orton had no such marks, but had a scar as if a piece of skin had been removed. He had originally had his own initials tattooed there and had made a clumsy effort to have them excised before attempting to claim the inheritance.

In 1935, an extraordinary coincidence occurred in Australia, linking tattoos with murder. A shark was captured and sold to an aquarium, where it promptly vomited up a human arm, which had been severed with an instrument, not bitten off by the shark. The skin carried a distinctive tattoo of two men boxing. A police search into missing persons soon came up with a tattooed man and the design was recognised by relatives as belonging to a James Smith. This was confirmed by finger-printing and an acquaintance of Smith was eventually charged with his murder. The coincidences did not stop there, as a star witness was also murdered before he could give evidence!

Another type of individual stigma may be of help, not in establishing the personal identity, but in suggesting the probable occupation of the deceased. In the past, perhaps too much weight was given to such hints, though maybe it was more justified in those days of more manual skills in various trades. Thickened skin or callouses may be seen on the bottom edge of the hand in clerks or draughtsmen, on the fronts of the shins in men who spend a long time on ladders (such as painters), on the front finger and thumb pads of bricklayers (though they may even get thinning of skin on the left hand from constant abrasion with bricks). Barbers, laundry-workers, carpenters etc. may all get various callouses, but it is too much to depend seriously on these features, except to say that the deceased did some form of manual work. More specific pointers are found in certain trades — the coalminer invariably has 'blue scars' on the arms, hands or face, where coal dust has penetrated minor cuts and lies like a tattoo beneath the skin. Steelworkers and blacksmiths frequently have multiple tiny scars from splashes of hot metal. Photographers and chemical workers may have stained, distorted nails from the action of chemicals.

Of more use is non-medical scientific evidence gleaned from the clothing. The forensic scientist may learn a great deal about occupation from true-life Sherlock Holmes examination of the dust from pockets and turn-ups. This is even more important in non-fatal crimes associated with robberies, but in all sorts of investigation, the examination and analysis of various metal dusts, shavings, earth, chemicals and stone-dust from the clothes can assist in identification. Special small vacuum-cleaners may be used by the scientist to retrieve such silent witnesses. The dust is sucked up into a special chamber containing a fine filter which traps the dust for examination.

Returning to personal identification, scars are another important means of putting a name to the unknown body. These may be scars of old injury or those from a surgical operation. Often the latter are more useful, as they may be recorded in old hospital notes and be exactly documented both by position and age. Other useful types of scar are those which develop on the skin of the abdomen of pregnant women. They usually persist after childbirth and help to establish the fact that the deceased had been pregnant at some time.

Scars go through a spectrum of colour changes which may help to date them very approximately. At first, they are red or blue and slightly raised above the surface. Later, usually after many months, they contract and become hard and silvery, often sinking slightly below the level of the surrounding skin. After a year or so, they stop altering and remain static for the remainder of the life span.

In what is probably the best-known murder case in British criminal history, that of Dr. Crippen's killing of his wife, identification was one of the most important and most controversial aspects of the trial. All that remained of the alleged Mrs. Crippen was some decomposed soft tissues hidden in lime beneath the flagstones of the cellar floor in the Crippen household. All the bones and head had been removed, the only useful evidence being the isolation of a poison (hyoscine), some hair and a four-inch scar on a piece of skin. This was examined by Bernard Spilsbury and said to be an operation scar on the abdominal wall, consistent with the fact of the deceased woman having had her appendix removed, a fact which was known to be true.

The defence denied that the skin was abdominal or that the mark was an operation scar; their eminent medical witness maintained that it was a crease due to the skin being folded during burial, but Spilsbury satisfied the jury that the absence of hair roots or sweat glands in the mark indicated that it was a scar. The arrangement of the muscles below the skin indicated that it came from the abdomen, in his opinion.

It was this case that really launched Spilsbury into the forensic limelight, which he was to dominate for so many years.

All types of physical abnormalities may be of great assistance in identity, such as the abnormal tendon bone mentioned below. Harelips, club-feet, old amputations of limbs or fingers, old fractures seen on X-ray, diseases of joints, skin ailments and of courses, moles and birth-marks all are heaven-sent gifts to investigators stuck with an unidentified body. But these are relatively rare, or, even if present, may not clinch identity if no one can be found to vouch for them on some missing person.

Surgical operations and congenital abnormalities can be very useful as a means to identification. In that classic case of Ruxton, the wife's remains had evidence of a bone deformity due to a bunion; the murdered maid showed removal of skin from the forearm in order to hide a birthmark and a localised excision of part of the thumb drew attention to the fact that efforts had been made to remove an old scar.

A woman's body was recovered from the River Tyne during cold weather. It was dressed in night attire and was in a moderate state of decomposition. Around the neck was a leather belt; the ankles were tied together with string and wire. Both the belt and wire had empty loops suggesting that weights had been attached but had come loose.

Enquiries amongst missing persons lists suggested that the woman might have vanished from Sheffield six weeks before. The husband, a detective-sergeant, viewed the body but denied it was that of his wife. However, a son said that it was his mother.

Identification now became of the utmost importance, as post-mortem examination had revealed that death was due to asphyxia from strangulation. After removal from the water, the features rapidly deteriorated and other methods of positive identification were sought. The presumed identity was eventually substantiated in three ways; the woman had been involved in a road accident about a year before her death and had been admitted to hospital. Comparison with the hospital records confirmed what were small scars on the knees from the accident; her gall-bladder had been removed some years before and the dead body had no gall-bladder and an operation scar in the appropriate place; lastly, X-rays taken at the time of the leg injury showed an unusual bone in the Achilles tendon of the heel. On X-raying the body from the river, an identical bone was discovered.

After a two-week trial at Leeds Assizes, the jury agreed that identity was proved and also convicted the husband of murder.

An interesting 'stranger-than-fiction' aspect of the case was that the husband was held to have driven the body the hundred-odd miles from Sheffield to Tyneside in the back of his estate car during a foggy night. Half-way along the Ai trunk road, he crashed on to a roundabout in the fog and buckled a wheel. Whilst helpless there, a police patrol arrived and, suspicious because of many night robberies in the area, flashed their torches into the back of his car and saw a long object wrapped in sacking. The husband diverted them by producing his own police warrant card, and the police then assisted him to move his car to be repaired so that he could continue his mission!

A far more useful factor in most cases is the state of the teeth — so much so that in recent years, a whole new speciality has arisen, that of forensic odontology, the legal aspects of teeth. This is a province of dentistry and often a member of a university dental college takes a particular interest in the matter so that police and pathologists can consult him over any dental aspects of a case.

Mention has already been made of the dental contributions to estimating the age of an unknown corpse. One of the great advantages of dental evidence is that it is just as useful when the body has been reduced to a skeleton, depending only on the presence of dentine and enamel, the constituents of teeth which outlast even bone in survival time. Much of the anthropological advances of the antiquity of man have been made on teeth, as they are so resistant to decay. Teeth have already been mentioned in connection with ageing, but here the determination of *individual* identity is discussed.

Few people nowadays go through life without visiting a dentist and dental records are kept in most cases from schooldays. Any extractions and fillings are noted at each visit and so a dental 'map' exists of a large part of the population. The accuracy with which these records are kept varies with different dentists, but especially since the National Health Service started they are becoming more complete.

When a body is discovered and all normal means of identification fail, a detailed survey of the teeth is made. All missing teeth are noted, the number, position and nature of fillings described and the presence of decay, cavities and any particular features like bridge-work, capped teeth or gold teeth recorded.

The next problem is finding a match for these; very often, one or more presumptive identities are available for the body and when this is the case the dental records of each suspect are compared with the details of the unknown corpse. The vast number of permutations of extractions, fillings etc. in thirty-two teeth run into astronomical figures, and there is usually no doubt at all when similar features are present in both records and dead body. The main sources of difficulty in this technique are the lack of records with which to compare, the inadequacy of a record when it is available and out-of-date records. Even so, dental examination can be vital and sometimes is the only evidence of identity.

The importance of teeth in identification is illustrated by a case occurring in Mid Wales during a recent hot summer.

A car was found abandoned in a remote area near a large forestry plantation. The car had no number plates nor licence, but tracing the engine number via manufacturer and dealers, the police found that the last owner was a retired senior Army officer living near London, some 200 miles away. A search of the forest was made and eventually a body was found, in an advanced state of decay. The pathologist called to the scene found the corpse to be virtually a skeleton inside a suit of clothes. The skull was separated from the body and showed an obvious through-and-through gun-shot wound. Under the body was a German 9-mm. Luger automatic pistol. There w ere no papers or other identification on the body and the police were naturally very suspicious that this might be murder. The officer who owned the car was known to have been alive three weeks before and, considering the very advanced state of decay of the body, it was felt that this could not be the same man. Memories of the Rouse case, where impersonation of a man in a car, murdered for insurance money, made identification an urgent matter.

Failing any ordinary police methods, the only lead was the teeth, which had a great deal of dental work, including gold bridge-work, an artificial tooth and numerous fillings and extractions. Enquiries were made at hospitals who dealt with service personnel and dental records of the missing officer were obtained. They agreed in no less than twelve separate places with the teeth of the unidentified body, apart from one extracted tooth which must have been removed recently. Even dental X-rays were available from the hospital and were exactly comparable with X-rays taken of the dead man's teeth.

The reduction of a body to a skeleton within three weeks is an example of the great variability of decay relative to climatic conditions and illustrates that dogmatic statements by doctors can often be shattered by the exceptions to almost all rules.

Another classic in homicide identification occurred during the forensically difficult days of the last war. Now known as the 'Baptist

Church Cellar case', the trial of Harry Dobkin took place at the Old Bailey in 1942, for the murder of his wife.

During bomb damage clearance, remains of a corpse were found beneath the flagstones of a church in Kennington, London. The body had been crudely dismembered and buried in quick-lime (a popular fallacy exists that lime hastens decay, whereas, in fact, it has exactly the reverse effect). The head was separated from the body and parts of the limbs were missing. The larynx and womb were present, but most tissues useful in identification (face, eyes, lower jaw, hands and feet were gone). The height was calculated from the left thigh-bone and found to be between 5 feet and 5 feet 1 ½ inches. The age was estimated from the fusion of the skull bones and other factors, as being between 40 and 50. A few' strands of hair were found, of dark brown and grey colour. The body had been partly burned, but the uterus could still be seen to contain fibroid tumour.

The upper jaw contained a few teeth and their fillings and roots were recognised by a dentist, who also pointed out thickening of the jaw-bone resulting from some other dental work. He described the condition of the teeth before even seeing the specimen and further forecast correctly that roots of two teeth would be found in the jaw, where they had broken off during extraction. The woman in question had also been diagnosed as having a uterine tumour, for which she refused operation. A photograph of the woman, Mrs. Dobkin, was obtained and was found to have no points of dissimilarity when superimposed on a photograph of the skull from the chapel. A haemorrhage was found in the lining of the larynx and the cartilage was fractured, indicating that strangulation was the probable cause of death. The husband, Harry Dobkin, was found guilty of his wife's murder.

In the notorious 'acid-bath murders' committed by John George Haigh in the years preceding his trial in 1950, the identity of the last victim was obtained largely by dental evidence. She was a rich widow', Mrs. Durand Deacon; her only remains consisted of some fatty sludge, a gallstone and an acrylic plastic denture. The last was positively identified by her dentist.

Dental evidence is particularly useful in the event of a mass disaster, such as aircraft or rail crash. Where severe injuries, dismemberment, mutilation and fire make identification of numerous casualties almost impossible, the comparison of dental records with remains is sometimes the only hope of sorting out the deceased.

Apart from the major roles of establishing age and personal identity, dentists have helped in a few cases to solve crimes not always associated with death. This has concerned the matching of bite marks, either on substances at the scene of a robbery or on the skin of the victim of an assault or rape.

Tooth marks on cheese, fruit, butter and chocolate have been sufficiently clear to make a plaster or acrylic cast for permanent record — even the slight indentations on skin can be recorded in cast form with certain techniques. Close-up photography is also carried out and if a suspect is found, his own teeth may be compared in a similar way with the marks found at the scene of crime.

Children and young persons tend to have grooves on their teeth which will make a particular indentation on a bite; these smooth out in later life, but all types of irregularities from spacing, chipping and disease may impart a characteristic bite mark.

*

One further technique remains to be described in connection with the identification of skeletal remains. If the skull is available as well as a photograph of the face of a possible candidate for identity, attempts may be made to match the two. The procedure calls for expert photography, as the skull must be photographed at exactly the same angle and magnification as the available snap-shot. A negative of the skull on transparent film is then carefully superimposed on a print of the photograph and when satisfactorily adjusted, reference marks are made on each picture to retain the alignment. Then various points on the skull and face are compared, making allowance for the thickness of soft tissue. The eyebrow ridges, the bridge of the nose and the point of the chin are particularly important, as well as the ear-passage and the tooth line, where visible.

This technique is considered only to be an *exclusory* method in Britain; in other words, if the reference points do not coincide, then this is definite evidence of non-identity. If they are a good match, then this is a good confirmatory pointer, but by no means conclusive without other evidence.

In the Soviet Union, the Forensic Research Institute in Moscow claims to be able to make a *positive* identification, rather than merely an exclusion. They have a vast experience of comparing skulls and photographs, due to the exhumations that have been necessary from the thousands of victims of Nazi atrocities and battle casualties. The Russians have also pioneered another technique of reconstructing facial appearances by building up the skull with pads of clay, the thickness being determined by the bone structure beneath. This combination of art and science has been used to restore the features of famous men of history, such as Ivan the Terrible.

In conclusion, it can be said the establishment of identity can be one of the most arduous, yet most satisfying, of forensic tasks and one which is as vital to the prosecution as establishing the cause of death itself.

SIX — ASPHYXIA

Once upon a time, in the days of the classical forensic authors, everything was simplified and all deaths from pressure on the neck and other means of cutting off the air supply were called 'asphyxia'.

Nowadays, we know that things are not nearly so simple and the old black-and-white descriptions have merged into all shades of grey. Nevertheless, true asphyxia still commonly occurs and the typical features will give us a base-line from which to compare the other things.

Body cells need oxygen to live. Without it, they die at varying speeds according to their degree of activity and specialisation. Brain cells become sick and die within a few minutes of being deprived of oxygen. Heart muscle, kidney and other organs can stand a much longer oxygen starvation but become irreversibly damaged after an hour or so. Inactive tissues like skin and fibrous tissues can survive much longer, but of course they are doomed if oxygen lack kills the brain centres that control breathing or the heart muscle that maintains the circulation.

Oxygen reaches the cells of the body by transport within the red blood cells, which use haemoglobin as a temporary carrier. Air is pulled down into the lungs by the action of the breathing muscles of the diaphragm and those between the ribs. It distends the spongy air-spaces of the lungs and passes through the thin filmy walls into the blood which percolates between the spaces. The oxygen is taken up by the haemoglobin and carried to remote tissues, where it is given up. On the return journey, the blood brings back carbon dioxide, the main waste product of the cells, which is then vented into the lungs and blown out when the breath is exhaled.

Strictly speaking, asphyxia can occur anywhere along this complex chain of oxygen transport. The oxygen can be prevented from passing across the thin walls of the air-spaces if they are damaged by irritants, like ammonia gas or certain rare diseases of the lung. More commonly, the red-cell transport system fails, as in anaemia, where the cells are fewer, and after severe haemorrhage when again the number is reduced.

The number may be normal, but the oxygen-carrying capacity may be reduced, as in coal-gas poisoning. Here the carbon monoxide snaps up all the haemoglobin and prevents the oxygen from getting a place inside the red cell.

Next, though oxygen gets through the lungs and into the red cells, failures of circulation stop the cells getting to their destination, the so-called 'stagnant asphyxia'.

Finally, even if oxygenated red-cells arrive at the tissues, the body cells may not be able to use it, as in cyanide poisoning, where the cytochrome enzymes which utilise oxygen are knocked out of action.

Though all these catastrophes are 'asphyxia' in the physiological sense, the forensic meaning usually refers to an earlier stage — that is, when air is mechanically prevented from getting down to the lungs.

The lungs are supplied with air via a wide tube, the windpipe (trachea), which stretches from the Adam's apple (larynx) down to the middle of the chest, where it divides into two smaller tubes (bronchi), one for each lung. The trachea and bronchi are rigid, being kept open by ladder-like rings of stiff cartilage.

At the top end, the larynx or voice-box is a rigid structure containing the vocal cords. Between it and the roof of the mouth is a horseshoe-shaped bone, called the hyoid. Behind the trachea and larynx runs the gullet (oesophagus) and at the top of the larynx is a springy flap called the epiglottis, which prevents food from falling down the air-passages. All these structures are important in the pathology of asphyxia.

Cutting off of the air supply, though having the same final result, is classified in forensic practice according to level of the obstruction.

Blocking of the outer end of the system is termed 'smothering' or 'suffocation', blocking of the tubes by something stuck inside them is usually called 'choking', while squeezing of the windpipe by external force is called 'strangulation'.

Suffocation can have many causes, some criminal, others accidental (or even suicidal). Deliberate criminal suffocation is relatively rare, usually occurring in children or old people. A pillow pressed hard across the face of a baby or frail octogenarian may be enough to cause asphyxia without any struggle, but the same procedure would be very difficult in a robust adult. Victims of epilepsy sometimes die from asphyxia if they have a fit and roll on to their faces in a soft pillow, when no one is at hand to clear their 'airway', as free ventilation is called.

This mechanism was once thought to be the cause of death in the mysterious 'cot death' condition, but this will be fully discussed in the chapter on infant deaths.

Deaths from suffocation have sometimes occurred during robberies, where a watchman or shopkeeper has been trussed up in best gangster fashion and a cloth tied either around the face or only across the lips. Even if the nostrils are left clear, the accumulation of saliva and phlegm may eventually block the back of the throat and after the robbers have left, the victim may die of asphyxia. The thieves may then be technically guilty of murder, even though a death was far from their minds; in practice, a manslaughter charge usually rests.

Suffocation is often further sub-divided into 'smothering' which describes the external obstruction described above, 'choking' which refers to internal blocking of the air tubes by some foreign object and true 'suffocation', often by smoke or other non-poisonous gas which cannot support respiration.

A new form of smothering has been seen in recent years — the plastic bag. Many fatal accidents have occurred in infants, who pulled such bags over their heads and died very rapidly. Even plastic sheet, not in bag form, can cause death in small children. It can cling very tenaciously to the face (possibly due to some form of static electricity) and block the nose and mouth. Death has been seen to happen so quickly that a pure asphyxia is sometimes in doubt; the mechanism is obscure and may be related to carbon dioxide retention or that vague but over-employed diagnosis of 'shock'.

Plastic bags occasionally are instruments of suicide, being either secured under the chin by a cord or neck-tie or left loose, when they still cause asphyxia. A gas-pipe may be led underneath the bag, when carbon monoxide poisoning competes with asphyxia as the cause of death.

In adult males, plastic bags may be involved in the peculiar sexual perversions described in another chapter and deaths in these circumstances are accidental, not suicidal.

Smothering or suffocation may occur when a person falls into a large volume of powdery substance such as sand, grain or any finely divided material. The usual place for such accidents are hoppers full of dust, corn etc. in factories or farms. A common cause for such tragedies are attempts to clear an obstruction in the hopper; the contents cave in and the air passages and mouth of the victim may be filled with the substance, which can flow almost like water. The mechanism of death may be complicated by the presence of 'traumatic asphyxia' described below.

Choking may be from a variety of causes. Ramming a gag into the mouth during robberies may be one, part of the gag going right back to the upper air-passages. Much more often, choking is accidental and, like so many other mishaps, is much more frequent at the extremes of life, especially in the mentally deficient. Mentally defective children may push foreign objects down their throats or eat with such animal enthusiasm that pieces of food may jam in their air-passages. One such child was asphyxiated in a tub of pig-swill kept outside the kitchens of a large mental hospital. Similarly, senile old persons, especially in institutions, may eat so ravenously that they block their windpipes and die rapidly. Often, the true nature of the death is unsuspected until the post-mortem. One old lady was found to have a complete rolled-up pancake standing on end in her windpipe and discoveries of large masses of meat or bread are not uncommon.

Small children are at risk with small playthings and should be strongly discouraged from an early age from putting such objects in their mouths. Ball-bearings, plastic toys and all manner of things can impact in the trachea and cause death. A rapid opening of the windpipe with a penknife or razor blade may be the only hope of survival, but it is rare for someone with the knowledge or initiative to be available in the few minutes before death. Peanuts are common things to be inhaled, but their size usually allows them to go right down into a lung, where they rarely cause death, but may give rise to serious lung complaints.

Asphyxia may occur in its most florid form, not from any obstruction of the air passages, but from mechanical restriction of the breathing movements of the chest. This, for no very good reason, is called 'traumatic asphyxia' (trauma being a more exotic word for injury) and often displays the most gross signs of asphyxia at post-mortem examination.

Most cases of traumatic asphyxia are accidental, due to some catastrophe immobilising the chest wall and bringing normal respiration to a halt. The only record of its use in homicide is is in the notorious 'resurrection men', Burke and Hare, who are said to have procured bodies to sell to the Edinburgh Medical School by sitting on their chests to stop them breathing!

The accidental cases most frequently arise in workmen who are partly buried by falls of sand, rubble, earth, grain, gravel etc., which, although it may leave their nose and mouth clear, effectively prevents the indrawing of breath. A common tragedy of this type is the collapse of a trench due to inadequate shoring-up of the sides, which give way and trap men working below. The same may occur in roof-falls in coal mines and in large hoppers or silos in factories and farms.

A less common but equally tragic cause is the crushing that may occur in uncontrolled crowds.

During a mass 'walk' for charity in the North of England, a false start was made and a stampede began in the entrance of a football ground where the walk was to begin. Several persons were knocked to the ground and one unfortunate female student suffered extreme fatal traumatic asphyxia due to the pressure of the crowd around her.

Many of the deaths in the similar tragedy at the Bolton football ground were due to this type of asphyxia, as were most of the 173 deaths in a London tube station, used as a shelter during the air raids of the last war. The 1971 Ibrox Park disaster was similarly caused,

The same phenomenon may be seen in some traffic accidents, especially tractors, where an overturned vehicle pins down the chest of the driver.

Traumatic asphyxia exhibits such gross changes that this might be an appropriate point to describe the typical features common to all cases of asphyxia before going on to the more frankly criminal causes.

Most of the changes are due to lack of oxygenation of the blood following prevention of access of air to the lungs, but also to a sudden rise in the pressure in the veins. The last effect is particularly marked in strangulation, as the constriction of the neck dams back the blood into the head by blocking the normal drainage via the veins.

Both these results of asphyxia lead to a deep flushing or congestion of the skin, especially in the face and neck. As the blood is not oxygenated, the haemoglobin of the red cells cannot be converted into the usual bright pink of oxy-haemoglobin, so the blood in the swollen veins is dark, giving a purple or blue tint to the lips, the face and often the fingers and hands.

The lining of the smallest blood vessels — the capillaries — is very sensitive to both increased pressure and oxygen lack. When these become deranged, the capillaries become fragile and burst at many points, causing small haemorrhages into the tissues, called 'petechiae'. The whites of the eyes, the eyelids and the lips are often peppered with small pin-head bleeding points beneath the skin. If the process is severe, as in strangulation or traumatic asphyxia, then they are also seen on the skin of the congested face and neck. Internally, these haemorrhages are even more readily apparent, so much so that they have a special name when found on the surface of the lung. They are then called 'Tardieu spots', after a Parisian police surgeon who described them in the last century. Unfortunately, they are not such an inevitable sign of asphyxia as was once thought (even Tardieu himself pointed this out). These little haemorrhages can occur in any congested condition without asphyxia and, conversely, true asphyxia can take place without them. But as a general rule they are of considerable use in confirming the mode of death, as long as their limitations are kept in mind.

Other possible signs of asphyxia, again common to any severe congestive process, are bleeding from the nose, mouth or even ear.

Moving down the air passages from the site of suffocation, we come to strangulation, the cause of asphyxia which has the main criminal connotations.

In the pure form, which is not as common as one might think, death is caused by typical asphyxia due to cutting of the air supply by squeezing the voice-box or adjacent windpipe. The squeezing may be achieved by pressure of a hand, which is 'manual' strangulation, or by the application of a length of any flexible material, then termed 'strangulation by a ligature'. All types of ligatures may be used, including rope, electric flex, belts, strips of cloth, stockings, ties, scarves etc. Accidental ligature deaths may be seen now and then, especially in infants, who get tangled up in their harness in a cot or perambulator. Sometimes, as in our fictitious case in Chapter Three, manual strangulation may be followed by the application of a ligature, either to 'make sure' or for other reasons.

Returning to manual strangulation, this common method of murder and manslaughter in Britain is usually accomplished by the forceful grasping of the throat of the victim from in front. If the assailant is right-handed, then a thumb will be pressed into the right side of the neck, the fingers on the left: the web of the thumb, where it meets the palm, will force back the middle of the neck where the air passage lies under the skin. The usual level for this attack is immediately under the skin either on, or just above, the prominence of the larynx, the 'Adam's apple'. The attacking fingers will bruise the neck below the angles of the jaw and the fingernails may cause typical semi-circular marks on the skin. There may well be other scratches and abrasions due to the victim frenziedly trying to tear away the assailant's fingers. The face and neck will be blue and congested, as already described and there may be bleeding from the nose. A shower of small haemorrhages may appear in the face and eyes.

Internal examination may reveal deeper damage under the external marks. The muscles of the neck commonly show bruising and bleeding, but the main changes are to be seen in the larynx.

The cartilage plates forming the front of the voice-box are rarely fractured (except in old age when they can be chalky and brittle) but at the upper end are two projecting 'horns' which lie below the horseshoe-shaped hyoid mentioned previously.

Both these horns and the thin ends of the hyoid may be fractured by the strangling hand and this is one of the main confirmatory features sought at autopsy. In youth, these horns on both larynx and hyoid may be so soft and supple that they merely bend under the assailant's fingers and spring back when released. In adults they are usually bony and readily crack under pressure. They are so fragile that the defence may object that they were broken during the autopsy removal. To obviate this criticism, it is usual to look for haemorrhage around the fracture and even take tissue for microscopic examination in order to prove that the crack occurred during life. X-ray pictures of the larynx may also be of great help at autopsy, as they show up small fractures difficult to see with the unaided eye.

As well as these characteristic fractures, the inside lining of the larynx and air-pipe may show extreme congestion and haemorrhage due to direct squeezing. The root of the tongue may show very severe congestion and possibly haemorrhage.

The rest of the examination is unhelpful in strangulation, except to confirm gross congestion and the presence of the common tiny haemorrhages in the chest organs. The scalp often reveals widespread haemorrhage, which must not be confused with direct head injury.

Strangulation with a ligature offers the additional evidence of a circular mark around the neck in place of the finger marks, though skin damage due to the victim trying to pull it off may be present. The nature of the mark naturally varies with the type of ligature used. A rope or thick cord will usually leave a good imprint on the skin, indicating the type of surface of the ligature. A woven or plaited rope will leave its pattern in either scraped skin or lines of tiny haemorrhages. A fabric may leave the imprint of warp and weft; a recent case showed a perfect imprint of a thick-knitted pattern from a woollen polo-necked jumper, when the neck was squeezed by an encircling arm.

The width of the ligature mark on the skin may be totally unrelated to the width of the ligature. Wide bands of cloth or stocking commonly leave a narrow band, which may lead the inexperienced eye to think a rope has been used. It is the taut ridges of material that leave the lines, not the unstretched remainder of the cloth on each side.

Strangulation by a ligature is less likely to fracture the larynx and hyoid, partly because it tends to be applied lower down than the fingers, which slide up under the chin, and partly because a ligature has a wider area of contact, so that pressure is not focused into a few particular spots.

The descriptions above refer to uncomplicated asphyxia where death is due to obstruction of the entry of air. In practice, many cases are not so simply explained, because another factor operates in addition and may entirely replace the asphyxial element. This factor is pressure on the large blood-vessels of the neck, particularly the carotid arteries, which run up on either side of the windpipe to carry blood to the brain.

Whereas 'pure' asphyxia would take several minutes to achieve death, the majority of strangulation deaths die more quickly than this and a considerable proportion are virtually instantaneous. This is due to the attacking fingers or ligature causing pressure on the carotid arteries and stopping — or greatly reducing — the blood flow to the brain. Unconsciousness occurs within seconds of the brain being deprived of blood. The combination of asphyxia and deprivation of oxygen to vital brain centres which control breathing and heart-beat, can hasten death very markedly, before the full-blown features of asphyxia can appear in the skin and organs.

Taking this a stage further, sudden 'grabbing' of the neck can cause immediate death. Many times, a typical story has been heard from a husband who, in a fit of temper during a domestic squabble, seizes his wife around the throat to shake her, with not the slightest intention of killing her. "She went limp under my hand" is the oft-repeated description and certainly, the death *can* be that sudden, with no possible time for asphyxia to occur.

That a carotid reflex can cause instant cardiac arrest is amply borne out by the case where a woman dropped dead whilst dancing, in full view of a roomful of witnesses. Her soldier partner had merely tweaked her neck with his fingers in affectionate playfulness.

The complete absence of signs in death from pressure on the neck is emphasised by the recent murder of two small boys in Newcastle upon Tyne. The first, a 4-year-old, was found dead minutes after being seen near derelict houses due for demolition. He was found dead in an empty room, with nothing to explain the fatality. Apart from a faint bruise on the head, there were no marks or injuries. Empty medicine bottles were present in the house and for a time this was thought to be the most likely cause of death, but analysis of samples from the autopsy were negative.

No suspicion of foul play was aroused and an open verdict returned by the coroner. Angry residents of the area marched to City Hall to demand demolition of the dangerous houses, but several months later, another small boy was found strangled nearby and this time suspicion fell on two girls, aged 9 and 10. They were brought to trial on a murder charge, evidence being given that they had broken into a nursery school to leave threatening obscene notes, had openly boasted about being responsible for the first boy's death and had raised fears in the minds of senior police officers that they might repeat the killings. The older child was acquitted, but the younger one found guilty of murder, being only 10 at the time of trial.

The explanation is that the carotid arteries have small swellings on them at about the level of the voice-box, which are very sensitive to changes in pressure. Their normal function is to act as pressure gauges, sending messages via the vagus nerve in the neck to the brain and heart, in order to maintain a steady blood-pressure. If they are grossly over-stimulated, as by a punch, they will become frantically over-active and send out an explosive set of nerve impulses which can stop the heart in its tracks. This is the object of the Commando punch and various karate chops, which are directed to these spots on the carotid arteries with the intention of causing sudden, silent death.

In the Emmett-Dunne case, the deceased sergeant was found hanging by his neck from a staircase, but he had livid staining of his face and shoulders, whereas, if he had hanged, it should have been in the lower part of the body. Evidence at the court-martial indicated that after the accused had killed him with a throat-punch, the dead man was left face down either on the floor or on the ground for more than half an hour.

This mechanism of carotid stimulation is a 'reflex', as the nerve impulses flash from the artery to the brain and back to the heart. Before the mechanism was properly understood, the term 'vagal inhibition' was commonly used, to account for all sorts of sudden death where no apparent cause could be found. Deaths can occur from severe fright, from falling into cold water, from touching the neck of the womb during abortion attempts and many other apparently non-mortal acts.

Emotion, apprehension, and outright fear appear to increase the risk of this Vagal inhibition', and it will be mentioned again under appropriate sections. Unfortunately, the term Vagal inhibition' fell into bad odour some years ago, as it was unsubstantiated by any scientific proof and tended to be used indiscriminately. As the common end-result to a variety of over-active nervous stimuli is stoppage of the heart, a better term might be 'reflex cardiac arrest', though the difference is only one of semantics. Certainly, it is of great importance in any discussion of assaults to the neck region, as probably the majority of strangulations and hangings have at least an element of reflex cardiac arrest to complicate — or even replace — the asphyxial element.

HANGING

Suspension by the neck naturally has a great deal in common with strangulation with a ligature, but there are important differences.

Firstly, of course, hanging is almost never homicidal (with the major exception of judicial execution, which is a totally different mechanism!). Most cases are suicidal and a number are accidental. In the typical hanging suicide (like shooting, almost exclusively confined to males) a rope, cord or wire is looped around the neck, either with a slip knot or a fixed knot. By some means, either all or part of the weight of the body is allowed to fall on the ligature, so that strangulation occurs. Like the other forms of strangulation, death may occur from pure asphyxia, pure vagal arrest of the heart or from a combination of both.

Due to the mechanism of hanging, the ligature rides much higher up the neck than in homicidal cases, lying immediately under the chin in front. The slack of the rope rises in an inverted V either to the back of the neck or more often, to one side behind the ear. In either case, the structures in the upper part of the neck are forced upwards and part of any asphyxial element is due to the base of the tongue being rammed against the back of the throat. Due to the high position of the rope, the horns of the larynx and hyoid are not often fractured. A deep groove is seen in the skin, usually parchment-like and stiff in texture when the rope is removed, due to friction and pressure on the upper layers of the skin. Like the murderous ligature, the same pattern of rope or wire may be deeply imprinted into the tissues.

Though the suicide may often arrange things so that he hangs with his feet above the ground — usually by kicking away a chair or box — this is by no means necessary to accomplish a rapidly fatal result. It has been calculated that a tension on the rope need only be eight pounds to block the carotid arteries and this can easily be achieved by considerably less than full suspension. The practical proof of this is seen in the numerous cases where suicides have been found on their knees on the floor, their heads attached to a door knob or even sitting down alongside a bed-post to which a noose has been tied.

Accidental hanging occasionally occurs in some industrial situation where a workman becomes entangled with ropes and sometimes in infants who become suspended on their perambulator harness. A further few instances have been seen in older children who attempt to emulate the lynching of cowboy films, but these are sometimes difficult to distinguish from the accidental hangings of masochistic sexual perversion. Here it is sufficient to emphasise once more that these are *accidents* and not suicides, as is sometimes still recorded by coroners unfamiliar with these bizarre exercises.

Judicial hanging is neither asphyxia nor carotid pressure, but a gross mechanical injury causing dislocation of the spine with rupture of the spinal cord and instant death.

DROWNING

Dead bodies are recovered from the water very frequently in this country. As will be seen, convincing proof of actual drowning is not always forthcoming, but coroner's verdicts of this mode of death amount to over 1,500 a year, two-thirds being accidents. The rest are suicides, as murder by drowning is extremely rare, though the disposal of bodies in water after homicide is well known.

The forensic examination of bodies recovered from water presents several particular problems. Often post-mortem decomposition is advanced and this makes both identification and the determination of the cause of death very difficult or even impossible.

The length of time that the corpse has been immersed is also a difficult question to answer, due to great variables in water temperature and contamination — very often, an experienced river policeman or 'longshoreman' may be more accurate in guessing this than a pathologist.

Determination of the cause of death may be very difficult even in a fresh body. Advanced post-mortem decay often makes it impossible for the doctor to offer a coroner an honest opinion and many death certificates have been filled in with the word 'unascertainable', unless there is other circumstantial evidence to satisfy the coroner.

The typical positive findings in drowning are well described in the text-books, but not often seen in practice. For many years, until research work into survival of crashed air-crews during the last war, it was accepted that drowning was another manifestation of *asphyxia*. Pathologists assumed the common-sense theory that if one fell into water and was prevented from breathing air, then death occurred from a watery form of suffocation. Yet the features of drowning in salt and in fresh water were different, especially the length of time of survival in each. Neither were any of the classical appearances of asphyxia found at autopsy — the congestion and haemorrhages were conspicuous by their absence.

It has since been discovered that, though oxygen lack naturally plays a part in death from drowning, the main cause of death is the fluid and chemical disturbances that rapidly take place in the blood.

When a person is submerged in fresh water, there is a preliminary period of initial struggling and panic, during which water is taken into the lungs. This comes into contact with the huge surface area (many hundreds of square feet) of breathing membrane, which is normally meant to deal with air. The blood on the other side of this membrane has a high content of salts and other body chemicals, so that by osmotic pressure, pint after pint of the fresh water is drawn through into the blood-vessels.

In a matter of seconds, the blood volume can rise catastrophically, so that the heart is unable to deal with all the extra fluid. The pump may fail at this early stage and death ensues. If not, further trouble is in store, because of the great dilution of blood chemicals (the blood volume may almost double). This dilution may lead to rupture of the red blood cells, as their thin envelopes cannot stand the sudden change in osmotic pressure. The red cells have a high content of potassium and when this is released in bulk into the blood plasma, it rapidly poisons the already over-burdened heart. Together with oxygen lack and accumulation of carbon dioxide which cannot be blow n off, the biochemical state of the body is in a sorry state within minutes, and death is then inevitable. This ability of the lungs to absorb great volumes of fluid may seem remarkable, but anaesthetists know that during long surgical operations pints of saline can be poured down the air passages to combat dehydration; and it vanishes quite satisfactorily.

Drowning in sea-water is somewhat different and offers a better chance of survival. When the water reaches the lungs, it already has about the same osmotic pressure as the blood plasma, due to the dissolved salts, so no massive fluid transfer takes place. In fact, fluid may be pulled out from the blood and lead to shrinking of the red cells, which does no immediate harm. There is some interchange of various chemicals, however, so that the sodium chloride (common salt) level rises in the blood.

These chemical changes have offered some diagnostic aid in drowning, but they are very limited in use. The body must be very fresh and more than twelve to twenty-four hours' delay makes the tests useless. The rationale of the tests depends on the fall in salt content on the *exit* side of the lung circulation in fresh-water drowning, compared with the salt content of the approach side. At autopsy, blood is taken separately from the left and the right chambers of the heart, and analysed for chloride levels. Both should be *low* in fresh-water drowning, due to the marked blood dilution, but that on the left side (coming *from* the lungs) should be the lowest.

In sea-water drowning, the sodium chloride level should be *higher* than normal in the blood coming from the lungs due to absorption of salt as the blood passes through the air-spaces.

The different mechanisms of death in the two types of water explain the common fact that death is far quicker in fresh water than in the sea and that recovery after prolonged artificial respiration is more likely to occur after sea-water immersion. Death is almost invariable after four minutes' immersion in fresh water but up to eight minutes in the sea. Much longer survival times have been recorded in the sea, up to twenty minutes and more, but usually this has been in very cold conditions where metabolism has been greatly slowed down.

At post-mortem examination the signs of drowning may be very slight, though evidence of immersion may be all too obvious.

The classical finding in drowning is the presence of fine froth in the air-passages and lungs, often foaming out of the mouth and nostrils. This is not unique to drowning, being seen in certain heart diseases. In drowning, it is due to the violent beating-up of water with mucus during the early stages.

The lungs themselves may be very much over-distended, filling the chest cavity so tightly that the markings of the ribs may be impressed upon them. The cut surface may be spongy and pour out water, as might be expected. Yet, more often than not, there is nothing in the air-passages and the lungs are dry, as all the inspired water has been sucked through into the bloodstream, giving the so-called 'dry-lung drowning' appearance. Unlike strangulation asphyxia, there are no Tardieu spots on the organs and no haemorrhages or dark congestion on the face.

Other signs, not directly related to the drowning process, may be found helpful at autopsy. The fingers may show 'cadaveric spasm', mentioned in Chapter Four, and in fact, drowning is the commonest time to see this fairly rare condition. Weeds or underwater debris may be grasped in the clenched fingers and may be helpful in reconstructing the circumstances of the immersion.

The air-passages may also have debris in them — weeds, mud, sand and other small objects. This is not an infallible sign of drowning, as things can float passively down the air passages after death, but a large amount of weed deep down in the lungs raises strong presumptive evidence of drowning.

The autopsy must include a careful search for causes of death other than drowning. Injuries are frequent on bodies recovered from the water, and many are post-mortem. These can be caused by the tide rubbing the body along the bottom, when damage to forehead, knees and arms is common. A corpse, after sinking at the time of immersion, usually hangs with the legs and head hanging down, so that post-mortem lividity is seen most strongly in these areas. After some time, dependent on the weather and temperature, gas formation due to putrefaction brings the body to the surface, where it floats usually in the same position, though an obese body with large fatty breasts or abdomen may float on the back.

Other damage may be caused by passing ships, especially in busy waterways like the Thames, Tyne or Mersey. Very severe injuries can be caused by propellers, and these have to be differentiated from the possibility of violence before death due to criminal action.

The problem of distinguishing between a truly drowned body and one that has been disposed of in water after murder on land, has been made easier by an elegant technique known as the diatom test.

Diatoms are microscopic water algae, tiny plants which have a hard, mineralised skeleton composed of silicates. They are very widely dispersed in nature, being in most pond and river waters, as well as different varieties in the sea. Unfortunately, they are often absent from polluted industrial waters and are also very scarce at certain seasons, especially in winter.

When a body drowns in water containing diatoms, these minute objects get sucked into the lungs and many of them penetrate the breathing membranes to gain access to the blood stream. During the few minutes before death, the heart pumps them around the body and they lodge in various distant organs. At post-mortem, with careful technique to avoid spurious dispersion, pieces of these organs, preferably liver, kidney and bone-marrow, are taken and dissolved in strong acid. This has no effect on the silicates of the diatoms and on microscopic examination, they can be seen in various organs. This confirms that immersion must have taken place during life and the case is not one of disposal of an already dead body.

If a dead body is immersed, then some diatom-containing water may percolate down into the lungs, and they can be recovered from here at autopsy. But as the heart is stopped, no diatoms can be carried to other organs.

This technique can provide useful information, as long as the water concerned has diatoms in it at the material time. In favourable circumstances, even the site of drowning can be determined, as fresh-water and sea-water diatoms are different and sea-water plants even vary from place to place along the coast.

*

In the 'Yacht Christine' case (R. *v.* Verrier, 1964), a man vanished in suspicious circumstances from a small boat in the English Channel.

A body was recovered many weeks later on the Belgian coast and identified by a surgical scar and fingerprints as the missing man.

In spite of gross decomposition, diatoms were recovered from many organs and were further shown to be of a type indigenous to the Kent coastline rather than Belgian waters.

All deaths from falling into water are not drowning. There is a well-known condition, loosely called 'shock' but better known as 'reflex cardiac arrest', which has already been discussed under asphyxia. The old term 'vagal inhibition' is the same thing and is frequently employed in those tragedies where a person is seen to fall into water and is pulled out immediately, before drowning could possibly occur — yet they are already dead.

This unfortunate phenomenon more often occurs in really cold water, during winter conditions. The unexpectedness of the event is a major factor, as with most 'vagal' reflex deaths. 'Shock' and 'fright' are everyday words to describe what happens — a case is on record of a practical joke where a youth was being ragged by others. They arranged a mock execution and told the victim that they were going to cut his head off. When they touched the back of his neck with a piece of ice to imitate a knife, he immediately died!

Similarly, the person unexpectedly hitting cold water can instantly die. A frequent predisposing factor is the intoxicated state of the unfortunate person. The classical situation is that of a drunken sailor coming back to his ship on a winter's night, and either staggering over the dockside in the dark or falling from the gangway. The effects of alcohol, either on the mental state or by flushing the skin and making it more sensitive to sudden chilling, appear to greatly increase the likelihood of immediate death.

Even when immersion is anticipated, occasional sudden deaths take place. The sudden impingement of cold water against the back of the nose or throat is believed to be enough to cause reflex cardiac arrest.

The 'Brides in the Bath' murders, a sensation during the years of the First World War, were committed by suddenly lifting the legs of the victim from the bath, allowing the head to slide under the water.

The cause of death of at least three women, wives of the notorious George Joseph Smith, was probably reflex cardiac arrest and not drowning. At the trial, the jury were taken from court to witness a demonstration; a nurse in bathing costume got into a bath and her feet were jerked up by a police inspector. She was immediately taken out, but had to be given artificial respiration to revive her — needless to say, the latter part of the demonstration was not intended, but served to impress the jury all the more.

In all these cases, none of the typical signs of drowning will be found, including a negative diatom test.

The lesson is that by no means all bodies taken from the water have drowned.

SEVEN — WOUNDING

Forensic pathology is largely the pathology of trauma and the study of the many types of wounds constitutes a considerable part of the subject.

Gun-shot wounds are dealt with separately, but here we will consider other injuries which may be seen in deaths from accident, suicide or murder.

An old legal convention, not formulated in any law, was that a 'wound' had to sever the full thickness of the skin. This is obviously untenable, as the most severe or even mortal injuries may frequently occur without a mark on the skin — a typical example is the ruptured spleen following a blunt impact on the abdomen.

A wound can be *any* disruption of the body tissues following violence, and the legal aspects are determined by the consequences of such injury and not merely by the local damage.

It is the job of the pathologist not only merely find the cause of death (which in severe woundings is all too obvious to the youngest police cadet), but to interpret the wounds to assist the investigators in reconstructing the assault and perhaps the sequence of events.

BRUISING

The most common wound is probably the bruise, also called a 'contusion' in medical parlance. A bruise is a haemorrhage beneath the skin due to the escape of blood from vessels, without any discontinuity of the overlying skin.

All grades of severity can be seen, from vague discolorations to massive purple blotches extending over many square inches. The apparent severity need not necessarily be related to the amount of force applied — old people bruise very easily and the merest touch may produce widespread extravasation of blood beneath their skin, which takes a very long time to vanish, should they survive.

The part of the body injured also makes a considerable difference to the extent of the bruising. Lax tissues such as the eyelids bruise easily, as in the common 'black eye', whereas firm, muscular areas like the thigh show little spreading of a bruise, and places like the sole of the foot or palm of the hand are almost impossible to bruise.

Bruises can arise from almost every sort of injury, and often accompany the other types of wound to be described later. They appear some time after the injury causing them, though this interval may vary from a few seconds to some hours when the person survives. The delay is due to the seepage of blood from the damaged blood vessels under the skin. Depending on the size of vessels damaged, whether it be tiny capillaries, small veins or arteries, the escape of blood will occur at varying speeds. If death is very rapid from other injuries, then the blood pressure will fall to zero and the leakage into the bruised area will almost cease, though a passive ooze may still occur after death, especially in dependent parts of the body. Faint bruises often become far more apparent some hours after death and the overall appearance of the injuries may be much worse after the body has been in the mortuary for a day or two.

Due to the diffuse leakage of blood beneath the skin, bruises are not very accurate indicators of the type of injury that caused them. Spacing of bruises may suggest a row of knuckle marks, for instance, but no sharply defined pattern can be expected as with abrasions on the skin surface. Occasionally, the weapon can be recognised as being a round rod, due to the 'tramline' effect.

Some rough indication of the age of a bruise may be gained, though no hope of accuracy is to be expected. A fresh bruise will be red or purple according to its size and depth. The haemoglobin of the escaped red blood cells begins to undergo chemical changes in the healing stages, if the person survives, and a brown colour gradually supervenes, which later passes through green and then yellow as it fades away.

The speed with which this occurs depends partly on the amount of blood present, but also on the state of health of the victim. Senile people have a poor capacity for absorption and bruises sustained in old age may last for months or even persist for the remainder of life. In healthy adults, bruises usually vanish within a few weeks but this is modified by their position and extent.

There has been some argument in the past, including legal argument in courts, concerning the possibility of simulation of bruising by post-mortem injuries. It must be accepted that these can be produced by very severe impact, especially in areas of hypostasis, that is, the livid areas of skin caused by gravitational settling of the blood after death. If the blood vessels are ruptured here after death, then some passive oozing can take place which is difficult to distinguish from ante-mortem bruising.

Sometimes, areas of this lividity may be mistaken for bruises; they can easily be differentiated by cutting into them, as the blood in true bruises is *outside* the blood-vessels, whereas in lividity, it remains *intra-vascular*.

Bruises are of particular value when found in certain sites at autopsy, especially on the neck, scalp and abdominal wall. Bruising on the neck is a characteristic sign of manual strangulation and may help to reconstruct the circumstances. A well-marked single bruise on the right side of the neck and multiple smaller bruises on the left strongly suggests a frontal attack by a left-handed assailant. Caution has to be exercised, however, to avoid the temptation of over-enthusiastic Sherlock Holmes deductions. The older school of forensic writers tended to read too much into many unreliable signs, and though being able to diagnose strangulation by a "one-legged, left-handed Chinaman with a glass eye and a wooden leg" is an obvious exaggeration, a firm check must be held on the imagination when called upon to interpret post-mortem appearances.

Sometimes, it is important to be able to differentiate post-mortem from recent bruises and the latter from older bruises. The first is difficult and only experience can help; subtle changes in colour and the slight swelling often associated with bruising during life may assist, but no really scientific tests are yet reliable enough, though enzyme reactions (mentioned later) hold some promise for the future.

Distinguishing bruises caused immediately before death from those of many hours' or days' duration is easier, though not always fool-proof. The later changes of colour have already been described, but these uncontrovertible signs of age do not appear for some days. A more sensitive method is microscopic examination. In bruises a day or so old, there will usually be an influx of white blood corpuscles coming to start 'clearing up the mess'. A few of these may even be seen in eight to twelve hours after infliction, though their appearance is too erratic to use as a means of timing.

ABRASIONS

Almost as common as bruises, the term 'abrasion' covers all sorts of superficial surface injuries which do not penetrate the full thickness of the skin. Scratches and grazes constitute most of the abrasions seen and are caused by tangential injury to the body surface. Bruises are also frequently present in the deep tissues, but abrasions are of far more use in reconstructing the type and direction of injury.

The causative agent can be almost anything with a sharp or rough surface from a pin or finger-nail to the gravel surface of a road. Road accidents often show the most widespread abrasions, where the body has been struck by a vehicle or thrown against the ground.

The direction of the injury can readily be determined by a close examination of this type of wound. If a weapon, such as a rough metal bar, has been used to inflict a glancing blow on the skin, then shreds of the upper layer of skin (the epidermis) will be torn loose and pushed or dragged along in the direction of travel of the weapon. At autopsy, these shreds will be seen sticking up at the end of the abrasion and common sense will at once indicate the direction of the blow. Conversely, where a body has been thrown from a car in a traffic accident and has skidded across a rough tarmacked road, the skin tags will be at the rear of the grazed lines on the skin.

Abrasions retain very fine detail, unlike bruises, and numerous instances of identification of a weapon or other injuring structure can be quoted. Before the front ends of motor vehicles became more sophisticated, the honeycomb pattern of the radiator fins was a common sight on a body. The tread pattern of motor tyres is sometimes seen on victims of traffic accidents. The notorious 'blunt instrument', beloved of crime writers, sometimes has some pattern that becomes imprinted on the skin, such as the circular embossing of a glass ashtray. Knuckle-dusters, toe-caps of boots, rings on fingers and even fabric patterns can be clearly imprinted on the skin and be of utmost importance as evidence in a criminal prosecution.

In the sadistic sex-murders of the Heath case, a perfect impression of a plaited leather riding switch was imprinted on the skin of one victim and assisted in matching the weapon with one owned by Heath.

Abrasions become more noticeable after death when the epidermis dries and the damaged parts become brown and leathery. This is particularly so in ligature marks seen in hanging and strangulation. These are also abrasions, caused by the friction of the ligature and again often show the pattern of the rope weave with faithful accuracy.

Abrasions may sometimes retain particles of foreign material which may further assist in interpreting the wounds. The long grazes of traffic accidents may contain road grit and primary injuries from vehicles may retain paint flakes or oil which may assist in identifying the vehicle in a 'hit and run' case.

WOUNDS THROUGH THE SKIN

Bruises and abrasions are useful signs, but do not in themselves contribute much to the actual death. Injuries of a severe or fatal type are usually those which penetrate the skin, though internal injuries to organs may occur with little or no external signs.

The first of these full-thickness skin injuries is the laceration. This is a tear through the body-covering caused by splitting of the tissues, due to impact either of the body against a surface or of a blunt weapon against the skin.

The characteristics of the laceration vary with the part of the body hit and with the nature of the offending object.

Where the skin is supported by a rigid structure beneath, such as the skull beneath the scalp, laceration is readily caused by a blunt blow and these may be so well defined as to resemble a wound caused by a sharp instrument like a knife or axe.

Where the underlying tissue is flexible, such as the soft parts of the limbs and abdomen, laceration occurs less readily and is often jagged and irregular.

These clean-cut splits of scalp or eyebrow can be differentiated from knife wounds by a close examination of the wound edges. Crushing will be visible and hairs will be bent into the wound. Bruising is often present under the margins and ragged tags of tissue will always be evident, especially in the depths of the wound. The nature of the weapon causing lacerations is often difficult to determine. Sometimes there may be 'tramline' effects where a rectangular bar is used, but round rods can cause identical appearances.

Again foreign material may be found in the depths of the wound and may help in identifying the cause — another illustration of the vital part played by co-operation between pathologist and forensic scientist at the scene of crime and subsequent autopsy.

The position of the lacerated wounds may be of great importance in reconstructing a crime. The angle and position of a blunt injury to the scalp may assist in determining the position of the assailant and the attitude of the victim. It may help to suggest which hand the attacker used, though again these interpretations must be made cautiously. Lacerated wounds of the scalp bleed profusely, and the consequent blood-spattering at the scene may also help to reconstruct the events.

INCISED WOUNDS

Sometimes superficially resembling certain lacerated wounds, incised wounds are made with a sharp-edged weapon and their clean-cut edges will be seen in whatever part of the body is attacked, not only over bony prominences. The incised wound is longer than it is deep — the reverse is true of stab wounds. Cuts made by axes, choppers and meat cleavers are usually on the scalp and are commonly homicidal in nature. The wounds from knives and razors usually occur on the face, neck and wrists and are not infrequently suicidal, though slashing of the face has unfortunately become more common in the gang fights of recent years.

Incised wounds tend to gape more than lacerations and they often bleed more freely, though fatal haemorrhage is relatively uncommon unless large arteries are severed, as in the neck.

It is very important for the pathologist to differentiate between homicidal and suicidal knife wounds. The cardinal point is the almost invariable preliminary attempts in suicide. The typical cutthroat of a suicide shows several (sometimes dozens) of tentative parallel cuts as he works up courage to make the final grand attempt. The same phenomenon may be seen on the wrists and even on the front of the chest over the heart. Not infrequently, these tentative cuts are present in suicides who employ some totally different method of killing themselves, such as poison or drowning — evidently the preliminary attempts have convinced them of the painfulness of the process.

The suicidal cut-throat is almost always recognisable by its direction. With a right-handed person, the slash will start high up on the left side and run down obliquely across the voice-box. The would-be suicide usually throws his head back, which tends to defeat his object, as this sends the great arteries and veins sliding back into the shelter of the windpipe, where the knife fails to reach them. Death may occur from slow bleeding from the tissues, sometimes complicated by asphyxia due to blocking of the cut windpipe by blood, but frequently the attempt fails or the sufferer kills himself in some other way.

The homicidal cut-throat, rarely seen these days, tends to be a single, much more savage slash, often at the side of the neck. No tentative wounds are seen and the presence of a single, severe incised wound always raises the presumption of murder.

The nature of the instrument cannot be gauged very well from long incised injuries. Where a blunt, wide-bladed weapon like an axe is used, especially if repeated blows have been inflicted on the scalp, recognition is fairly easy. But slashes with a sharp knife or razor leave no characteristics which would help identify the weapon, as they do in stab wounds.

Incised wounds can be caused by other things than knives. Glass is a common means, either as a deliberate weapon like a broken bottle or in accidents when window' glass can cause severe clean-cut wounds.

A particular case involving glass is the shattered windscreen of motor vehicles — here the driver and front-seat passenger often receive innumerable tiny lacerations of the face, due to fragments of the shattered windshield hitting them. As toughened glass is used in manufacture the fragments are relatively blunt and cause lacerations and abrasions rather than incised wounds, but the overall appearance is quite unmistakable.

STAB WOUNDS

Unlike the incised wound, the depth of the stab is greater than its length. In this fact lies the greater danger to life, as vital organs and blood-vessels are more likely to be injured. In incised wounds, though there may be a frightening amount of blood about, death is often due to other factors, such as head injury, unless a major artery is severed. Stab wounds may show very little external haemorrhage, but internal bleeding frequently leads to death. Most fatal stab wounds are of the chest and abdomen, though stabbing in the neck and groin can cause fatal damage to large blood-vessels.

The characteristics of the stab wound may provide a lot more information at autopsy than the incised wound. When a knife is stuck into the body and withdrawn, the appearance of the wound can help to reconstruct the attack, provided certain pitfalls are avoided. The width of the wound is usually *less* than the width of the blade, if the stabbing is a straight 'in and out' blow with no angulation or twisting. The smaller size of the slit in the skin is explained in two ways — firstly, as in the case of bullets, the knife causes stretching of the skin before perforation occurs. When the blade is withdrawn, the elasticity of the skin makes it spring back to its original dimensions, causing reduction of the size of the hole. Secondly, where a flat blade is employed, the wound will gape sideways on withdrawal of the knife, thus pulling the extremities of the long axis closer together.

The pathologist, then, must be aware of this and when measuring the length of the wound, be prepared to allow a little extra in suggesting the probable width of the knife.

Similarly, the *depth* of the wound may be fallacious, if the post-mortem distance be measured uncritically. The distance from the skin to the furthermost point of injury internally may be, say, 5 inches when measured at autopsy, but it is an unwarranted assumption to say that the knife blade must therefore be a minimum of 5 inches long. A forceful blow, such as may well have been delivered by the hand grasping the knife, can indent the skin surface several inches at the time of stabbing, especially in a pliable place such as the abdominal wall. Even the rib-cage can be 'sprung' inwards an inch or more with a heavy stabbing blow. Thus a blade of only 4 or even 3 inches can penetrate compressed tissues, which after recoil may measure 5 inches at the post-mortem examination. This naturally only gives a *minimum* penetration, no means being available to guess at the amount of unused blade, apart from possibly the width of the wound. In one case a bayonet was used to produce a fatal wound about 3 inches deep — the very wide skin slit suggested that a large weapon had been used, though a foot or so of blade never entered the body at all.

The shape of the blade can sometimes be suggested to the detectives by the pathologist. A dagger-like blade with two sharp edges tends naturally to leave a wound with clear-cut acute angles at each end, whilst a 'Boy Scout' type sheath knife, with a wide blunt back, sometimes carrying a serrated margin, will leave one sharp edge and one blunt or even torn extremity to the wound.

These are extremes and many blades leave little or no distinguishing features. The most common instrument of stabbing in recent years is the thin-bladed kitchen knife with a wooden handle. Though this sometimes leaves one blunt edge, the wound often exhibits no useful features.

Suicide and homicide pose the greatest problems.

The suicidal stabbing has declined greatly over recent years, as have all violent methods of self-destruction, due to the increased availability of poisonous drugs. Yet suicidal stabbings are seen from time to time, and there is a well-recognised pattern in the injuries. The tentative wounds of cut throat and wrists have been described already — the suicidal stabber usually confines his efforts to the front of the chest over where he imagines the heart to lie, or occasionally the stomach. Stabbing in any other part of the body must arouse the presumption of murder until proved otherwise. If the position of the wound is clearly inaccessible, such as the back, then homicide is confirmed forthwith.

Wherever mental abnormality exists, the stabbings and other suicidal woundings may be bizarre and very severe indeed — the genitals frequently come in for attack in these cases.

Multiplicity of stab wounds does not rule out suicide, even where each wound appears to be potentially fatal in itself.

In homicide, the site may be of utmost importance, as mentioned already. In addition, there are frequent wounds upon the fingers and hands, which at once confirm the murderous nature of the death. These wounds on the hands are called 'defence wounds' and are the result of the victim trying to ward off the assailant and even gripping the blade of the knife. They are often seen across the fronts of the fingers or palm, and sometimes on the back of the fingertips or even higher up the arm.

Before leaving the subject of knife wounds for good, one interesting type must be mentioned. These are invariably non-fatal and are neither attempted murder, suicide nor an accident. A number of cases are on record where a person has deliberately inflicted superficial knife wounds (or used some other sharp object) in order to substantiate a false story of attack by another party. These peculiar actions are usually to cover up some crime of theft committed by the same person, or to evoke sympathy for some ulterior personal motive. The nature of the wounds is often pathetically obvious, due to their regularity, their careful avoidance of vital or very sensitive areas of the body and their trivial depth. As life is never in danger, they are usually discovered by a clinical doctor or police surgeon, but in some police areas, the forensic pathologist has been called in, as this lies well within his experience of incised wounds.

HEAD INJURIES

Forensic pathology is largely the pathology of trauma and numerically, head injuries form a large part of the work.

The vast majority are accidental, but head injuries also account for a considerable proportion of homicides, especially those classed as manslaughter rather than murder. Head injuries cause many of the deaths from drunken brawls and affrays when some unfortunate is struck by brick, bottle or boot.

External head injuries have already been described under the sections on abrasions, lacerations and bruises. But the real danger lies not in these superficial injuries, grisly though they may appear, but in the damage to underlying structures of skull and especially brain.

The brain, the most complex and delicate of organs, lies well-protected in its strong bony box and the wonder of it is that it usually suffers so little damage in spite of the knocks and insults of life. To really damage the brain, a considerable force has to be applied to the head, though, as in all things medical, there are occasional exceptions to this rule.

The brain lies within three membranes inside the skull. The innermost is inseparable from the brain and forms its outer coat. Outside this is a meshlike membrane, the 'arachnoid', named after a spider's web. The outermost is the 'dura', a tough, leathery membrane which forms the lining to the skull. Between the membranes is a clear watery fluid, the cerebro-spinal fluid, which acts as a shock-absorber and allows the brain to move slightly within the skull. The adult brain weighs over 3 pounds and, being dense and heavy, it has considerable inertia, which is no advantage when the head is subjected to violent movements. At the lower end, the brain is continuous with the spinal cord which passes out through the large hole at the base of the skull and passes down the spinal canal. The brain is 'anchored' at this point, a factor of some importance in the mechanics of brain damage to be discussed below.

When the head is struck a heavy blow, a variety of effects may occur. The skull can be fractured and the nature of this fracture depends on the nature of the striking object.

A very localised impact, such as the head of a hammer, will cause a circumscribed fracture, sometimes depressed below the level of the surrounding bone. The shape of the fractured area may correspond with the shape of the weapon, though more commonly, the bone shatters into fragments. Radiating lines may spread out to a considerable distance and the overall effect is referred to as a 'cobweb fracture' from the obvious similarity.

A more blunt impact over a wide surface area will cause linear fractures, either single or multiple, which can travel for many inches across the top of the skull-cap and into the base, which forms the floor on which the brain lies. This is the most common type and is seen where the head hits a hard surface, as well as the famous 'blunt instrument' hitting a stationary head.

Fractures of all types are dangerous for several reasons. They are associated with brain damage, but not necessarily the cause of it, both things being caused by the force applied to the head. In addition, they can produce severe bleeding inside the skull from rupture of blood vessels. There are arteries running in grooves on the inner surface of the skull, which supply the meninges (the membranes mentioned earlier). Where a fracture crosses an artery, there can be a break in the vessel, with consequent outpouring of blood into the space between the bone and the membrane. This is called an 'extra-dural haemorrhage' and is a common sequel to severe head injuries of all types. It is particularly dangerous as there is commonly a period of normality after the injury before the blood has had time to accumulate in any quantity. This may lead to the victim thinking that he has no serious trouble or to a doctor or a hospital discharging him as fit, when in fact he later goes into coma and dies. The condition is eminently treatable by a relatively minor brain operation, which makes the tragedy of a 'missed' brain haemorrhage all the more unfortunate. Many a manslaughter or even murder charge has been brought after these haemorrhages, which might well have been avoided if diagnosed early.

Brain damage in head injury is a very complex matter and one that is not perfectly understood even now.

Where skull fractures are gross, the underlying brain may be severely lacerated and pulped. The mechanism here is not obscure, but severe bruising and tearing is often seen with small fractures or even no fracture at all!

The answer lies in the delayed response of the brain to rapid acceleration and deceleration, due to its inertia.

Where a fixed head — such as one lying on the ground — is struck a violent blow or kick, the part struck will show a laceration or bruise of the scalp, probably a fracture of the skull and bruising of the brain surface. All these injuries will probably be in roughly the same place, as might be expected.

Yet if a person is knocked down or flung over, so that his head falls violently against the ground or some other hard surface, then there will be a scalp injury and a skull fracture at the site of contact, but the brain injury will be *diametrically opposite*!

This phenomenon is called 'contre-coup' and is of fundamental importance to the forensic pathologist when examining fatal head injuries.

It was formerly thought that the 'contre-coup' injury was due to the brain bouncing off the opposite wall of the skull or due to a recoil of a shock wave travelling through the brain. It now seems probable that every head injury has a rotational element and there are shearing stresses set up due to the brain's inertia.

These account in part for the 'coup' injuries beneath the point of impact in the fixed head, but are magnified in the freely moving head so that the greatest shearing strains occur at the opposite pole, the 'contre-coup'.

For instance, where the left side of the back of the head strikes a kerb-stone after a push from an assailant, the direct impact contains some tangential component which rotates the skull with considerable acceleration. The brain lags behind, as it floats in its fluid buffer, but once its inertia is overcome, it also rotates around its axis on the spinal cord. When the skull comes to rest, the brain is still moving and now deceleration occurs. To these injurious rotational forces are added linear acceleration and deceleration, all of which combine to tear the attachments of membranes and blood-vessels and to compress and rarify brain tissue at the opposite end of the axis of movement, i.e. in this case at the right side of the *front* of the brain.

Just before closing time in a Welsh valley public house, a slightly inebriated young man suspected another of insulting his mother. Some time later, the second young man was found dead in the gutter, with a bruise on the chin, two black eyes and a cut on the back of the head.

The rapidly sobered assailant stoutly maintained that he had struck the victim only one blow on the chin, but a charge of at least manslaughter hung over him, until the autopsy. This displayed that there was a fracture of the back point of the head and severe 'contre-coup' injury to the front of the brain, resulting in bleeding into the eye-sockets, giving the impression of black eyes. This substantiated the stoiy of a single blow on the chin, with subsequent cracking of the back of the head on the edge of pavement.

Whatever the mechanics, the end result is of considerable practical importance to the pathologist at autopsy.

The relation of external bruise or laceration to the position of brain damage may support or disprove the story of an assailant. Where no story is forthcoming, the findings can help to reconstruct the fatality.

Other autopsy findings in head injury may be of similar evidential use. Confirmation of a high fall on to the feet may be obtained by the discovery of a 'ring' fracture around the entrance of the spinal cord; a fall on to the feet may cause fractures at either leg level, pelvis or skull, where the spine may be driven up into the head, leaving a ring defect in the bone.

Examination of the brain in a real or alleged head injury may reveal that death was, in fact, due to natural disease. A common condition in young and middle-aged adults, is the presence of a berry-sized swelling on one of the blood-vessels of the brain. This can burst either spontaneously or with rise of blood-pressure due to exertion or even emotion. It is a common cause of death in adult women, so much so that when a pathologist is confronted with the body of a woman between 20 and 50, he thinks first of some complication of pregnancy and then of a ruptured berry 'aneurysm' in the brain. Though these can burst with no predisposing cause, a sudden exertion like running or sexual intercourse can precipitate death. To these must be added any fight or physical disturbance, and a number of suspected manslaughters or murders have turned out to be natural deaths from this cause. Though the exertion and emotion of an assault or quarrel undoubtedly contributes, the connection is too tenuous to substantiate a criminal charge. The same holds good for coronary attacks during fights or family quarrels. Here again, the experience of a pathologist is vital to the full elucidation of a case and it would be a gross injustice not to have the benefit of autopsy findings where the possibility of a criminal charge may lie against some person.

EIGHT — SHOOTING

Though murder by gun-shot probably at once springs to mind when homicide is mentioned, this is more a product of the crime novel and television drama than a reflection of the true state of affairs in Britain.

Deaths from fire-arms are relatively rare in these islands, and those that do occur are usually from suicides and accidents, not murder. This is by no means so abroad and the number of deaths from homicidal shooting in the United States has now reached a level where it is becoming a problem which is disturbing the whole nation.

As an illustration of the difference, in 1966 there were a total of 143 murders in England and Wales, only twenty-seven of which were by guns. In the same period in the U.S.A., there were 11,606 murders, of which no less than 6,855 were caused by fire-arms!

Nevertheless, the total number of mortal gun-shot wounds in Britain is sufficient for the forensic pathologist to need a good working knowledge of the subject, especially in helping the police to come to some definite decision, when the circumstances are not sufficiently clear-cut to differentiate immediately between suicide, accident and homicide.

Though the actual examination of guns and their projectiles (often known, incorrectly, as 'ballistics') is the province of the forensic scientist rather than the doctor, the pathologist must have a good basic knowledge of the 'hardware' in order to interpret the wounds upon a body.

The nature of the injuries depends in great measure on the type of weapon used. These fall into two main classes, the rifled weapon and the smooth-bore. Injuries and deaths from the smoothbore gun are far more common in Britain than those from rifled weapons, mainly because the latter are virtually unobtainable, except in the small .22 calibre. This legal barrier to purchase accounts for the great difference in English and American death statistics, as the most lethal of weapons can be bought over the counter or even by mail-order in the States, with virtually no restriction. In Britain, smooth-bore shot-guns form the greater proportion of fire-arms available, as they are used for agricultural and sporting purposes. Permission to purchase is more readily obtained for these, though recently there has been a further tightening-up of the police regulations which limits their sale to more responsible people.

Basically, the smooth-bore gun consists of a wide metal tube attached to a wooden stock which contains the firing mechanism. Often there are two tubes side by side in the double-barrelled weapon. One has a slightly conical taper towards the muzzle, called the 'choke barrel', which has forensic implications, as will be seen later.

The width of the barrels varies — there is an archaic method of measuring them, which takes account of the number of balls of pure lead, totalling one pound weight, which would have the same diameter as the inside of the barrel. The commonest size on this scale is the 'twelve-bore'; the other common calibre is measured directly in inches and is called the 'four-ten', as its diameter is 0.410 inches.

The shot-gun fires a large number of small projectiles or 'lead shot', hence its name. These are contained in the cartridge, a cardboard or plastic tube with a brass base containing the detonating cap. The lower section is filled with explosive propellant, then comes a felt or cardboard wad to act as a piston. Above this, the cartridge is filled with hundreds of lead shot, the number and size depending on the type of ammunition. Finally, there are one or more cardboard discs to retain the shot, then the top end of the casing is crimped over the contents. All these components may play a part in helping the pathologist and scientific expert to reconstruct the shooting.

The lethal power of weapons loaded only with propellant and w ads is illustrated by several fatalities. In the Race case, a gun containing only paper wadding was fired from a few feet away and caused a fatal wound of the chest, the heart being penetrated by the paper.

A stage cannon, loaded with greased paper, blew away part of the hard of a spectator sitting in the gallery of the theatre.

When the trigger is pulled, a spring-loaded pin strikes the soft fulminate cap in the base, denting it and detonating the main propellant charge. This burns with explosive force and the contents of the cartridge are driven down the barrel and emerge at high velocity. What comes out is of prime importance for the doctor and forensic scientist. The lead shot, the flame, the hot gases (containing carbon monoxide), black soot, remnants of the explosive and the felt and cardboard wads may all contribute something to the investigation of the case. What is left behind is also vital to the scientist, if not to the medical member of the team. The spent cartridge — and of course the gun itself — may be paramount evidence to a conviction or an acquittal in a criminal case.

Rifled weapons are very different, both in construction and their effects on the human body. There are innumerable types, but those most commonly seen in civilian police practice are the pistols, either the 'revolver' or the 'automatic' (another misnomer, as they should really be called 'self-loading', a true automatic weapon being one which keeps on firing as long as the trigger is depressed). Less common, except in wartime, are the rifle and large automatic weapons, though they are still illegally possessed after theft from military sources. Thousands of 'souvenir' guns were loose in the community after the last two wars and even repeated amnesties have not cleared the country of them. At the last amnesty, incredible numbers were handed in, including large machine-guns and even an anti-tank 'bazooka'!

All rifled weapons have two characteristics lacking in the smoothbore gun — they all fire a single projectile and the inside of their barrel has spiral grooves cut in the metal, to give the bullet a spin when fired. This spin, up to 3,000 revolutions per second in a service rifle, has a gyroscopic effect and keeps the bullet on a steady path over long distances. The elevations between these grooves are called 'lands', and it is between the lands that the internal diameter of the barrel is measured. Common calibres are .32, .38, .45 and .303 of an inch, but metric sizes are becoming more common and are naturally well established on the continent, for example, 9 mm. The bullet is slightly oversize compared with the barrel, so that on firing, the softer metal is forced into the grooves to make a more effective seal against the propellant gas behind. This is called 'obturation' and is of vital forensic importance as the lands, which are never identical in any two weapons, gouge a characteristic 'fingerprint' on the bullet which assists in its subsequent identification.

Two types of pistol, mentioned above, have different methods of bringing a new 'round' of ammunition into the firing position and also a different principle of supplying force to the firing pin. The bullets and cartridge cases are also different and again all these factors have great significance to the investigators.

In the revolver, a rotating cylinder brings a new shell into line every time the trigger is pulled. The cartridges have a projecting rim at the base to grip the cylinder and the spent shellcases have to be removed manually after use. The bullets are usually soft lead, contrasted with the cupro-nickel casing of automatic ammunition. The speed with which the bullet leaves the barrel — the 'muzzle velocity' — is also much lower in the revolver, only about 600 feet per second, as compared with the self-loading pistol's 1,200 f.p.s. The service rifle may have a muzzle velocity as much as 3,000 f.p.s., the pressure of gases in the firing chamber being 20 tons to the square inch! These variations in energy profoundly affect the nature of wounds.

The 'automatic' pistol, the rifle and the machine-gun have their ammunition supply not in a revolving cylinder, but in a spring-loaded magazine. This is a metal box containing the cartridges lying on top of one another. In the automatic pistol, this lies in the handle, on the rifle it clips in front of the trigger-guard, and in the various types of 'machine-gun' it can occupy a variety of positions.

In the rifle, the new round is pushed into position by the action of a bolt, which manually extracts the last used cartridge at the same time. In the self-loading and truly automatic weapons, this manual act is replaced by mechanical power derived from part of the gas from the last discharge. This causes the empty shell-cases to be forcibly ejected, and they may land several feet away, either to right or left according to the type of gun. This aids scientific investigation, both by helping to determine the position of the assailant when he fired, the type and manufacturer of the gun and also in identifying the individual weapon, as each ejector mechanism leaves its own personal 'trade-mark' on the ejected shell-case.

Most of these aspects of the shooting are the province of the forensic scientist. Though most of the regional laboratories in Britain deal with such 'ballistics', any complicated cases are sent to the laboratory which specialises in this work, where a highly experienced fire-arms examiner uses his great knowledge on this very complex subject.

To return to the medical aspects of shooting fatalities, the pathologist himself has a series of complex questions to answer: WHAT TYPE OF WEAPON WAS USED?

This is usually one of the easiest questions to answer, though sometimes at first glance the answer may be misleading. Examination at the scene of crime is often difficult; it may be pitch-dark, with only torches as a means of lighting. The body may be in some inaccessible place or covered with something in an attempt at concealment. Though eventually the truth will be apparent, initially the recognition of the type of wound may be difficult. A small-bore shot-gun, such as a .410, may leave a hole resembling a large-calibre pistol. Once the body has been removed to more suitable surroundings, and certainly at the autopsy examination, the type of gun is rarely in doubt for long.

A shot-gun wound on the skin at anything but very close range, will be immediately recognisable by the 'peppering' effect of multiple pellets, in contrast to the single hole of a rifled weapon. Internal examination will reveal the widespread scattering of these tiny lead balls, many flattened and distorted by contact with bones and other body structures.

The single bullet of the rifled weapon is often found in one piece, though it may be badly distorted by hitting bones etc. The common exception, of course, is where it completely traverses the body and emerges on the other side. Then the presence of two holes leaves no doubt as to the type of weapon, as shot-guns rarely produce through-and-through wounds, unless in a narrow part of the body like head, neck or limb and then only from close discharge. Sometimes a large bullet may completely disintegrate on contact with bone, but the jagged fragments can never be confused with shotgun pellets.

Ideally, all shot-gun injuries should be X-rayed before the post-mortem starts, to gain an idea of the position of the projectiles in the body. This will immediately clinch the nature of the weapon and also indicate the amount of dispersion of pellets or the site of single or multiple bullets. It can be exasperating to try tracing a bullet without X-ray and many forensic pathologists can remember frustrating hours in the middle of the night, looking for a projectile that eventually turns up far away from the expected position.

FROM WHAT RANGE WAS THE FATAL SHOT FIRED?

This is often a very important matter to be settled early in the investigation, as suicide can usually be eliminated if the distance can be shown to have been greater than arm's length. Even here, some suicides have created problems in this context, either wilfully or accidentally, by rigging up devices that will fire the gun from beyond arm's length. This is usually done in order to fire a rifle, Where the trigger may be out of reach. The absence of a weapon naturally rules out suicide, but even this has been a red-herring on exceptional occasions.

Normally, the determination of distance is easier with a shot-gun than with a rifled weapon. The mass of shot leaving a smooth-bore gun diverges in a cone-shaped manner, so that the greater the distance, the wider the pattern of pellet wounds. At very short distances, however, other factors are important. Where the gun is pressed against the surface of the body, there may be a circular bruise on the skin from the violent recoil of the muzzle. There will almost certainly be a jagged hole left, with split, stellate margins due to gas erupting from the tissues. This gas contains carbon monoxide, which is described in the chapter on poisons. This combines with the haemoglobin of blood and muscle to form a cherry-red compound, which may be recognisable to the naked eye and detectable by spectroscopic examination of the tissues under the skin near the wound.

A body recovered from water several weeks after death was due to carbon monoxide in an advanced state of decomposition, but pink discoloration (confirmed by spectroscopy) existed in a circle around a gun-shot wound of the chest. In spite of the decay, this gave excellent confirmation of a contact discharge.

Both contact wounds and short-distance discharges may show' other characteristic features. The flame from the muzzle may scorch the skin up to about 3 feet distance with a shot-gun, but only a few inches with a pistol. This is modified by the type of weapon and the presence of clothing over the injured skin surface.

As well as the flame, soot and particles of unburnt pow der are throw n out and caught in the weave of the cloth or 'tattooed' into the skin. This is not so noticeable in these days of modern 'smokeless' powders, but is still often a prominent feature of shot-guns and revolvers. Some of the almost microscopic flakes of unburnt powder may be recovered from the skin or clothing by the forensic scientist and identified with a particular brand of propellant or matched with ammunition still in the possession of a suspect.

The mass of shot emerging from a shot-gun holds together in a compact mass for a variable distance after leaving the muzzle. A single large hole is made at very close ranges, perhaps up to a couple of feet or even more, but after a yard or so satellite pellet holes begin to appear around the margins of the main hole. As the distance increases still further, the holes become more numerous and widespread and the central aperture diminishes and finally vanishes altogether.

A well-used, though inaccurate formula is employed to calculate the distance of the muzzle from the skin. The range in yards is taken to equal the diameter of the pellet pattern in inches less one, so that a peppered wound 8 inches across would have been made by a shotgun discharged at about 7 yards distance. This very approximate rule-of-thumb is further complicated by the fact that smooth-bore guns have barrels of different types — cylindrical, half-choke and full-choke. The latter two are slightly funnel-shaped, being narrower at their muzzle ends. This naturally converges the shot more and a full-choke barrel gives a dispersion of about a quarter less than the half-choke, and even less again than the cylinder, which is usually on the right-hand side of a double-barrelled shot-gun.

Yet another source of inaccuracy to the 'yards equals inches' rule is the type and condition of the cartridges. Different-sized powder charges, qualities of propellant, size and quantities of shot all vary the divergence, as does the age of the ammunition. Old cartridges tend to clump more than new and some sportsmen (and poachers!) deliberately tamper with their ammunition. In the north of England, there is a practice of removing the top of the cartridge and pouring in candle-grease or even pitch! This causes the shot to coalesce into a lump that would stop an elephant in its tracks and makes a nonsense of the 'yards-inches' rule! Fortunately for the pathologist, these freaks are relatively rare in human gun-shot injuries.

Burning hairs may persist up to about 3 yards, in diminishing degree as the range increases. On hairy parts of the body, only semi-microscopic 'clubbing' of the tips of hairs might be seen, though chemical evidence of powder staining and residues may be obtained from skin and clothing. The use of infra-red photography may reveal powder residues that are invisible to the naked eye.

With shot-guns, the felt or cardboard wads that act as a piston may be of further help in determining the range. Again, there may be great variation according to circumstances, but the wad is rarely found deep in the wound at ranges over 6 to 8 feet, though it may travel in free flight up to 20 feet in certain cases. Its presence in the body normally suggests a fairly close discharge.

Death from a shot-gun varies according to the part of the body hit; close discharges to the head or trunk can be grossly destructive and rapidly fatal, but the lethal nature of a smooth-bore drops off sharply as the range increases, unlike a rifled weapon. At ranges over 30 yards there is unlikely to be a fatal outcome, unless some particularly vulnerable part, like the eye, is entered by pellets.

Rifled weapons are designed to be lethal at far greater ranges, and death from a military rifle can occur at well over a mile. At close ranges, the characteristics of the rifled weapon wound are very much like those of the shot-gun. Contact wounds will produce a muzzle bruise, carbon monoxide staining and splitting of the tissues from erupting gases. Powder blackening is seen at close ranges, though this is usually much less prominent due to the cleaner nature of the propellant. Burns and hair-singeing are also a feature of the near discharge, but again over a much smaller distance than the shot-gun.

At distances further than a couple of yards, it is almost impossible to determine the range, as there is naturally no divergent pattern of shot, only a single entrance hole. This often shows a stained margin, due to dirt and grease being rubbed off the bullet as it passes through the skin, but this is of no assistance in telling the distance. The hole is often smaller than the diameter of the bullet, as the skin is elastic and recoils after denting and stretching from the passage of the missile. A fairly close discharge may cause a wider hole and a wider track through the body, compared with a more distant firing. This is due to the instability of the projectile during the first few yards of its flight, before it settles down to a steady gyroscopic spin. In this early stage, there may be 'tail-wag' — that is, though the nose follows the strict line of flight, the tail revolves in a small circle around the axis of travel. This soon settles down to a straight path, but at the end of its travel, the bullet again becomes unstable as momentum is lost. Its flight becomes irregular and it may wobble wildly, even turning head-over-heels. A wound inflicted at these extreme ranges can cause a very jagged injury, which may be confused with a near discharge or even a shot-gun wound, unless other factors are taken into consideration. All these snags make the estimation of range of a rifled weapon rather difficult, except when fired within a few feet of the body. Of course, the presence of ejected shells at the scene may at once assist in the determination of range, but this is a matter for the detective officers, not the doctor. FROM WHAT DIRECTION WAS THE SHOT FIRED?

Again, this problem is more easily solved by the pathologist when a smooth-bore weapon is involved, especially with near discharges. At short range, the gun leaves a large hole with possibly a few satellite pellet holes, but in addition there is the burning and powder-tattooing. This at once points out the direction of the discharge, as there is rarely an exit wound with a shot-gun and even if there is, it can never be confused with the entry wound, though sometimes it can be mistaken for other types of injury.

Distinguishing entry from exit wounds — and hence the direction — where rifled weapons are involved is usually straightforward, but can be difficult when a high-velocity bullet enters from a distance. There are then no powder marks or burns, and the missile, if it misses bone or hard tissues, will pass cleanly through the body. Under these circumstances, the entry and exit wounds will look very similar, but close examination will invariably distinguish them. Though both wounds will be clean-cut and small, the edges of the entry wound will tend to slope inwards and the exit will gape slightly. A grease-collar from the bullet may be seen around the entry, though if it has passed through clothing first, it will have been wiped clean; even then, the grease may be detected on the cloth and fibres from the cloth may be carried into the entry wound.

Most fatal wounds from rifled weapons will show such easily recognisable features to determine the direction of travel, that the proverbial 'policeman's grandmother' could tell the answer, without the help of a pathologist! A small wound, perhaps smaller than the bullet calibre, marks the point of entry, and a ragged, everted hole, many times larger will gape at the site of exit. The main reason for this large hole w here the missile emerges, is the disturbance to its flight caused by structures in the body. Even if it does not hit bone, solid organs like the liver and heart can distort its pathway and make it wobble and stagger so that the track is markedly widened. If bone is struck, as in the case described below', then fragments may accompany the missile and further enlarge the exit or even make separate escape holes.

Two boys were playing with their father's loaded shot-gun on the stairs of their home in a northern county. The gun was accidentally fired at about 3 yards range and the younger brother was hit in the neck. A typical entrance wound was caused, but on the back of neck were two cleanly incised wounds looking so much like knife slashes that the police were suspicious of some criminal complication. Autopsy soon revealed that these wounds were due to fragments of spinal bone *emerging* after being hit by the mass of lead shot.

The angle of firing may be almost as important as the general direction when the circumstances are being investigated.

In determining the angle, close discharges are again the easiest to interpret. The powder marks will be circular if the muzzle is held at right-angles to the skin, but elliptical if the gun is held obliquely, the long axis of the ellipse increasing with increasing obliquity of the barrel. This is often seen in suicidal injuries to the temple, when the gun is held at a slope alongside the ear. Similarly, the pellet pattern in a shot-gun will form a circle or an ellipse, depending on how tangential the cone of shot is to the body surface.

The edges of the actual bullet hole, with rifled weapons, also give a clue as to the direction. A circle indicates a perpendicular discharge, but an oval wound with an unevenly bevelled margin gives away the obliquity of the axis of the bullet.

At autopsy, the direction of the track of the bullet or shot also indicates the angle, though caution has to be used in allowing for deflections by bones and organs. The pathologist also has to remember that the position of the deceased when shot need not be upright and unless he allows for this, some injuries would appear to be indictable only from a passing aeroplane!

In a recent shooting in a lonely house in the Forest of Dean, the victim suffered a shot-gun wound from several yards range, which entered above the left collar-bone. The face and chest showed an oblique pattern indicating that the direction of the shot had come from a high angle slightly to the left of the deceased. At the trial of another man, who had vanished after hiding the body under the kitchen table, the defence tried to assert that the dead man had been shot in self-defence from a vantage point on a low wall. Unless the deceased had been leaning forward in a most unlikely posture, this was impossible and, in fact, the shot was fired from a bedroom window down at the victim on the path outside.

Where a shot enters the skull, it is easy to determine the direction and angle. The bones of the cranium are in the form of a 'sandwich', with an outer and an inner layer of thin hard bone on either side of a central soft core. When a bullet passes through, it punches a clean hole in the outer layer, but as it leaves the inner layer, it shatters it and forces the fragments in the direction of its travel. Consequently, a missile passing clean through the whole head leaves a dish-shaped crater on the *inside* of the entry hole. The same is sometimes seen on the *outside* of the exit hole, but more often, this is completely shattered, though the inner hole may be cleanly punched.

The track of a bullet through the body is almost invariably much wider than the diameter of the missile. Due both to the wobble and to the enormous compression forces that are exerted sideways, the pathway of damage is often three or four times as wide as the bullet, especially in solid organs like liver or brain.

The destructive power of some military weapons causes injuries that resemble explosives rather than gun-shot wounds. An example is the NATO rifle, the 'F-N' (Belgian Fabrique Nationale) which uses a long cartridge and has a very high muzzle velocity. A female terrorist in Malaya, hit in the ear by a single bullet from this weapon, suffered complete disintegration of the head reminiscent of a grenade injury.

Experiments have been made by firing bullets into blocks of gelatine and the effects recorded by high-speed cine photography, the film running at 8,000 frames per second. The passage of the bullet is followed by severe transient 'cavitation', a wide vacuum track, which pulsates before dying down in a few milliseconds, leaving a narrower permanent track. It is this rapid lateral transfer of energy that causes most of the damage.

In passing, it might be mentioned that some relatively low-powered air-rifles are by no means toys and several fatalities in children have been recorded in recent years — so much so that since 1962 it is illegal to give or sell one to a child under 14 and no one under 17 may carry an uncased gun in a public place.

THE NUMBER OF SHOTS

One further question remains for the pathologist at the autopsy on a gun-shot death. How many times was the deceased hit? This is usually obvious, and almost always only one discharge has caused the death, but occasionally awkward cases present themselves.

It is rare for two bullets to pass through the same entry hole, but very closely placed shots may be confusing, especially if there is only one exit wound. X-ray or extensive searching at autopsy will clear up the question. The presence of three holes can be confusing; it usually occurs when one bullet has passed right through, while a second has been stopped by bone. Very rarely, there may be two entry wounds and a single large exit hole where the converging missiles have both left together.

Having determined the type of weapon, the range, the direction, the angle and the number of shots fired, the duties of the pathologist are not yet over. The actual manner of the death must be determined — this naturally depends on the part of the body hit. Head wounds usually cause severe brain damage and wounds of the chest or stomach cause laceration of major organs with massive bleeding into the body cavities.

It is most unsafe to dogmatise on the rapidity with which even severe injuries may cause death. Sir Sydney Smith reported a case in 1943 where a man shot himself in the mouth with a large-calibre Colt automatic. He did this in a shelter, upon the ceiling of which were later found fragments of bone and brain. Notwithstanding this, the man walked a few hundred yards home in the snow, rang the bell, spoke to a servant and walked upstairs, where he survived for three hours with a gaping hole in his head and brain.

Many other apparently mortal injuries have been survived or even unrecognised. A mental patient in a Welsh hospital once pestered the medical staff for an X-ray of his head, and when eventually they took one to humour him, they discovered a nail-file lying completely embedded in the brain, after the patient had quietly pushed it through his skull by mere thumb pressure.

An even more extraordinary illustration is that of the quarryman whose head was transfixed through the frontal lobes by a crow-bar hurled there by a blasting explosion. Surgical removal was successful and no apparent ill-effects occurred.

The time taken to die must be estimated, though this is a question fraught with pitfalls. A more immediate job at the post-mortem is the collection of evidence for scientific examination. The bullet from a rifled weapon must be sought and recovered with great care. The identification of the actual weapon used may depend solely on the individual markings on the bullet, so any heavy-handed treatment by the doctor may ruin the best evidence for the prosecution — or defence. That is why X-rays are so useful. They can pin-point the position rapidly and accurately, avoiding lengthy and blind searching, which may lead to the missile being irreparably damaged by a sharp instrument during autopsy.

Once located, the bullet must be gently removed by finger-tips or forceps with rubber-covered tips. On no account must a bare metal instrument be used, especially with a soft lead missile like a revolver bullet. Once safely removed, it must be carefully wrapped in cottonwool in a container for safe transit to the laboratory; rattling about in a bare glass bottle for a 100 miles does nothing to clarify the rifling marks on a piece of lead!

In shot-gun wounds, the recovery of pellets is not so useful as finding a bullet, but as many as can be found are taken, though it is a physical impossibility to recover even the major part of the hundreds present in the average cartridge. Nevertheless, the pellets can be useful for determining the weight and size, which may be matched up with a certain type of ammunition still possessed by a suspect. The actual chemical composition may also help in comparison work of this kind.

The clothing and the skin around the wound are carefully preserved, as they may have powder flakes or burning which will help both in range determination and in comparison studies with various types of propellant powder from suspect ammunition. As mentioned earlier, the examination of the tissues around a wound for carbon monoxide may help to confirm a close-range discharge and differentiate between entry and exit wounds.

All these minute bits of evidence are carefully preserved and labelled, as well as all the rest of the usual samples taken at a criminal autopsy.

When the post-mortem examination is completed and the evidence collected, the pathologist has to make up his mind about the nature of the death. He is often pressed for an immediate answer at the mortuary, as the investigating detectives naturally want to get on with the job. A massive murder hunt costs money and man-power, and in doubtful cases the responsibility of letting loose a murder squad on the area may rest heavily on the pathologist's initial decision. Though in many cases, the circumstances are obviously indicative of accident, suicide or murder from the outset, there are other cases where the decision is far from being clear-cut.

The extreme importance of examining gun-shot wounds before interference — as with all medico-legal autopsies — is emphasised by the Merret matricide in Scotland in 1926.

John Donald Merret was tried the following year for the shooting of his mother with a .25 pistol. The death was assumed at first to be suicide, though these are rare in women, but the forensic aspects were complicated by the washing of the skin around the wound in hospital, as the woman survived for some time. No record of powder burns etc., to confirm or disprove close discharge, was made. Spilsbury gave evidence for the defence and the accused was released on a Scottish 'Not proven' verdict.

Almost thirty years later, he murdered his wife, again trying to fake a suicide, then killed his mother-in-law who discovered the plot, before shooting himself.

Many pointers exist which help to make up the mind of the experienced pathologist — often they are almost intuitive and here lies the importance of the attendance of the forensic pathologist at the actual scene of the occurrence, wherever practicable. Even so, intuition will get short shrift from an astute defence counsel in a court of law, so the doctor must be able to back up his feelings with hard facts.

Certain definite factors are sought where the circumstances leave room for doubt.

Firstly, the absence of a weapon is crucial — apart from a few freak cases mentioned earlier, 'no gun means murder', or at least an accident followed by deliberate removal of the gun. Either way, a brisk investigation is called for. The only exception is a suicide or accident, where the deceased has managed to survive long enough to get well clear of the scene of the shooting. The severity of the injuries may exclude this at once, though some extraordinary instances of survival are on record.

The presence of two or more bullet wounds is also strong presumptive evidence of murder, as accidents and suicides are unlikely to display repetitive wounds, except where an automatic weapon is involved.

The presence of more than one potentially fatal bullet wound is suggestive of, but not absolute evidence of, murder. A case from Scotland reported five separate wounds from a revolver over a vital area of the chest, which was undoubtedly suicidal in nature.

Again, there are notable exceptions, but the general rule holds good that accidents and suicides are single-shot happenings.

The distance of the discharge is all-important. A gun fired from more than arm's length rules out suicide, unless some obvious mechanical apparatus is present at the scene.

A determined London man constructed a complicated wooden frame with an arrangement of levers which enabled him to commit suicide by shooting himself in the back of the neck!

Another perverse suicide, with an apparent grudge against the police, shot himself in a room immediately overlooking a river. He tied a cord to a stone and secured the other end to the trigger-guard of the pistol. By hanging the weighted end out of the window, the weapon was dragged from the room and vanished into the water as soon as his nerveless finger released their grip. The obvious situation of the room and the presence of scratches on the window-sill made the mystery a very short affair.

Self-destruction from long-barrelled weapons, such as rifles and shot-guns, is often achieved by using a stick to depress the trigger, but these will be even more obvious cases of suicide.

Of course, a distant shot may still be an accident, but this is a matter for the police or coroner to decide; unless the circumstances are transparently clear, the shooting will be treated as a murder until further clarification is obtained.

Other less obvious factors may help in distinguishing the three classes of shooting fatalities. It is a fact of life — or rather death — that women almost never shoot themselves. This certainly holds good for Britain and most of the Western world. All violent forms of suicide tend to be shunned by the female in Western society, though this is by no means so in Asia. In Malaya, young rubber-tappers crossed in love frequently drink acetic acid to kill themselves, this particularly nasty method being used as acid is freely available in the production of latex. In both the Middle and Far East, burning to death with petrol has been common for many years and has lately spread to Western countries as a result of the publicity given to Buddhist protesters in Vietnam. Potential suicides tend to be very imitative, and this is one argument in Britain for those who wish to see the coroner's inquest abolished — Press reports of inquests on unusual methods of suicide have more than once been followed by minor epidemics of similar self-destruction in the locality.

Returning to shooting, the most experienced pathologists are hard put to to recall more than a handful of women who have shot themselves, and a good rule-of thumb is that a shot woman has been murdered until proved otherwise! This applies equally well to accidents, as guns do not have the same fascination for the female sex as they do for young men. A large number of accidental shootings are seen in youths and men who delight in playing with guns and often participating in a near-masochistic 'brinkmanship' with loaded weapons.

Similarly, the part of the body injured is of great importance in deciding on the nature of the tragedy. Suicides are very conventional in the sites they select for the *coup-de-grâce*. The right temple (or the left in left-handed men), the left side of the chest and the roof of the mouth account for the vast majority of suicidal gunshot wounds.

In the political murder of King Ananda of Thailand in 1946, a rigged suicide failed because the site of election was wrong — the entrance hole was over the centre of an eyebrow, a very unusual position. There was a revolver on the bed where death occurred, but although of the right calibre, it was not the one that fired the fatal shot.

The eye and the stomach are almost never selected, though they are equally accessible — wounds of these sites and any other odd positions at once raise the possibility of murder or accident, as do wounds on inaccessible areas of the body. Naturally, a wound on the back rules out suicide, especially if a long-barrelled weapon is used.

Another test which has had a chequered career in reliability is the examination of the hands to determine whether they have recently fired a weapon. This can be applied to the hand of the deceased person to confirm a suicide or to the hand of a suspect who may have committed murder. The rationale of the test depends on the almost invariable leakage of gas from the breech of a gun when it is fired. The leaking gas deposits nitrates from the combustion of the propellant, on the skin of the person using the gun and sensitive chemical tests can detect this. Chemical reagents can be applied directly to the skin, or a paraffin wax cast can be taken of the whole hand, which is then opened out and tested for nitrates.

There are snags in this technique which have rendered it virtually obsolete, though it is resurrected now and then, especially by American criminologists. The first drawback is that many other substances give a positive reaction. Another is the length of time that nitrates may persist on the skin. A positive reaction may have nothing to do with the gun-shot that caused death, but may have occurred several days before. A test series has been described where frequent hand washing for nine days was still followed by a positive test. People who handle fertilisers, metal workers, photographers, engravers etc. may give a permanent positive reaction as a result of their daily contact with substances which give a false positive result. A negative test is fairly reliable evidence that a gun has *not* been fired recently, and from this exclusion aspect, it may sometimes be worth performing.

Where death is homicidal, and sometimes in an accidental shooting, a vital part of the investigation concerns the examination of the recovered bullets, empty cases and weapons. Though the pathologist's function here only concerns the safe recovery of missiles from the body, no account of gun-shot deaths would be complete without a mention of the techniques used by the forensic scientists in firearms examination. This task only passed to the scientists in relatively recent years. Forensic pathologists appeared literally 'on the scene' at least 120 years before the non-medical investigators in Britain — the first university chair of forensic medicine was established at Edinburgh as far back as 1805, the year of Trafalgar. The science of fire-arms examination was first developed by Professor Sydney Smith, a later incumbent of the same chair. In 1924, he had to investigate the political assassination of Henry Lee Pasha, Sirdar of the Egyptian Army, and comparison of revolvers and recovered bullets led to the conviction of the assassins.

The main purpose of this forensic 'ballistics' is to identify the weapon that fired the fatal shot. The actual make of weapon may be deduced from the type of ammunition and the rifling marks upon it. For instance, a soft lead -45 bullet will almost certainly have come from a revolver and if it shows six left-handed rifling marks, it may well have been fired by a Colt. This narrows down the search, though a vast practical knowledge and access to reference books is needed, as all sorts of inappropriate ammunition can be fired from various weapons. When a suspect weapon or weapons (sometimes scores or hundreds have to be eliminated) are obtained, then the vital question arises, "Was this bullet from the body fired from this gun?" or "Did this shell-case from the scene come from this gun?"

Even where no weapon is ever recovered, shell-cases can provide convincing evidence. In 1946 a woman was shot through the back of the neck with a projectile of 7.65 mm. calibre. A shell-case of Eley manufacture and of the same calibre was found near the body. The prime suspect had stolen a pistol of this size from an acquaintance some time before, and, though the weapon could not be traced, this acquaintance still had an empty shell-case, which he used as a core on which to wind insulating tape. Both this case and the one recovered from the scene of the crime had identical firing pin and breech-face markings and this, together with other evidence, was sufficient to convict Boyce, the main suspect.

With smooth-bore weapons, only the second is really capable of definite proof, though pellets from a shot-gun can be matched to the same *type* of ammunition as might be in the possession of a suspect.

It is the rifled weapons that provide the most profitable task for the forensic scientist. When a pistol or rifle is fired, the metal shell-case is forced violently backwards by the explosion and any irregularities on the face of the breech-block will be imprinted on the base. The impact of the firing pin will also leave a characteristic mark on the detonating cap (or rim, in the case of rimfire weapons like a .22). When the weapon is manufactured, machining marks on the pin and breech-face will never be identical in two separate guns and they will leave their 'fingerprint' on every round fired. Later damage or wear to the mechanism may cause even more marked idiosyncrasies — for example, the firing pin may get chipped or bent off-centre. When the cartridge-case is ejected, the violent movement of the ejector mechanism again makes a unique mark on the shell.

The bullet itself is usually the most important item in the investigation, though is often difficult to interpret, due to damage following impact. Occasionally, it is split or fragmented, and this makes comparison even less definite, though expert examination can usually produce some evidence of value.

When the weapon is fired, the bullet is forced from the firing chamber into the barrel, which is of slightly smaller diameter than the missile. This causes the softer bullet to mould itself into the grooves, which then imprint their pattern upon it. The grooves are cut in a long, shallow spiral and they vary greatly in number, size, pitch and direction with different manufacturers and models. For instance, most Webley automatics have six grooves with a right-hand thread, the Smith & Wesson 0.455 has five right-handed grooves and a Martini-Metford rifle has seven left-handed grooves.

Even more important than the identification of the type of weapon is the actual matching of the fatal bullet with the suspect gun. Apart from the pattern of the rifling, every gun has individual characteristics in its grooves and lands, due to tiny variations in machining during manufacture and also due to damage, dirt and rust which foul the barrel after purchase. This gives each weapon a 'fingerprint' of its own which is possessed by no other. Thus a bullet passing through a given barrel will acquire certain constant marks, which have been shown to persist unchanged, even though the gun may be fired many times.

To compare these individual characteristics, several rounds of ammunition, similar to that found in the body, must be fired from the weapon and recovered undamaged. This is done by test firing into a long wooden box filled with wadding or cotton-waste, which will arrest the bullet in a short distance without distorting it. Cards are usually inserted at intervals along the box, so that the task of finding the bullet is made easier by noting the last card to have a hole in it. Sometimes the bullet is fired into water, but precautions have to be taken to avoid dangerous richochets on hitting the surface.

Whatever method is used, the projectile is recovered along with the ejected cartridge-cases and these are examined by means of comparison microscopy and photography. This enables the test bullet and the bullet from the corpse — or two shell-cases — to be viewed simultaneously. Any similar markings are observed and photographed for production as evidence in court. The instrument used is a comparison microscope — a low-power version for larger objects is called a 'macroscope' — and really consists of two separate microscopes joined together by an optical bridge, so that half of both fields of view can be seen simultaneously in the eye-piece. Special mechanical devices hold the bullets or cases and these allow rotation and other movements so that similar markings can be lined up exactly for photography.

Other methods besides the comparison microscope are available. A special camera called a 'periphery camera' takes a single photograph of the whole curved surface so that pictures of each bullet can be laid side by side on the flat and compared for identical markings. Again, a gelatine cast can be made of each missile, which can then be opened out flat and photographed. Whatever method is used, the object is the same — to match up similar imperfections on the surface of the bullet or shell.

Comparison is by no means the sole function of the firearms examiner. His unique knowledge of weapons and ammunition may pin-point facts that may lead the detective team down fertile avenues of investigation. Abnormal types of ammunition used in a gun may suggest some particular suspect; the sequence of different ammunition in a revolver or automatic magazine may indicate the order of shots in a multiple shooting and elimination of certain types of weapon may cut down a widespread police search of a district.

One last detail — in many a novel and film, the detective makes great play of carefully lifting a murder pistol by a pencil pushed down the barrel, to avoid smearing fingerprints on the butt. This action would, in reality, give a forensic scientist grey hairs! Vital evidence may be dislodged by poking anything down the muzzle. Dust, cobwebs, rust or grease may indicate that the weapon has not been fired recently. Blood, clothing fibres and even skin fragments may show that a very near discharge occurred which blew back into the muzzle.

The proper way to lift a pistol — after it has been photographed *in situ* — is by twro fingers on each side of the chequered part of the butt or by the butt-ring, if there is one. However it is done, the investigator must make sure that it is not pointing at him or anyone else — some weapons found at scenes of fatal accidents have been so w orn as to go off at the slightest provocation!

Before the subject of fire-arm injuries is left, two other 'weapons' must be mentioned, being of some topical interest.

The first is the 'humane killer' used for slaughtering animals, which has turned up quite often as a means of human death. These are of two main types; one resembles a pistol, but fires a 'captive bolt', which is a metal rod that flies out of the barrel for a few inches, but does not separate from the weapon. It is powered by a blank cartridge, but naturally is as lethal to a man as to a horse or cow. Several suicides have been reported with these and one rather unfortunate accident, where a farmer, whilst attempting to kill a pig, shot himself in the knee and died later from tetanus infection (lockjaw). The other type of humane killer is a metal tube with a bell-shaped end which is placed on the animal's forehead. A live cartridge is placed in the other end and the exposed firing pin hit with a mallet. Again, several suicides have been committed with this device.

The other type of 'weapon' is the pistol used by building operatives to insert steel pins into masonry. They resemble the captive bolt pistol, but the pin is free. The muzzle is pressed against the wall for firing, but occasionally the pin ricochets off and can cause injury or even death at considerable distances. One case has been described where the pin penetrated a thin w all and killed a workman on the other side.

The use of blank cartridges in a humane killer raises the matter of the lethality of blanks. There is no doubt that they are highly dangerous and death has occurred in the absence of a bullet or shot. The explosive effects of the gas and the impact of felt w ads or other soft packing can cause severe injuries and death.

All too often in his dealings with accidental fire-arm fatalities, the doctor is struck by the total disregard for safety shown by many gun owners. Scores of small boys must have lost their lives over the years, because of their father's criminal negligence in leaving loaded weapons about the house. Farmers are particularly careless, and in addition many of their shot-guns are so decrepit that they will fire spontaneously when banged on the ground. Several farming fatalities have been seen where the foolish victim either used the loaded gun as a walking stick or employed the butt to prod a w ay through a hedge!

Familiarity may well breed contempt, but no one can afford to be contemptuous of a device that can convert a human body into bloody ruin in a fraction of a second!

NINE — DEATHS ASSOCIATED WITH THE REPRODUCTIVE SYSTEM

The title of this chapter presented some difficulty, as many 'reproductive' fatalities investigated by the forensic pathologist are not sexual crimes, nor are they all associated with pregnancy.

The first most serious criminal offence with a sexual aspect, is fortunately rare in Britain — the combination of rape and murder. Rape alone is by no means uncommon and from the medical point of view, this is the province of the police surgeon or female practitioner, not the pathologist. A careful history-taking, a full physical examination, retention of the clothing and samples from the genital passages constitute the functions of these doctors in order to substantiate the allegations, which are frequently false.

In fatal cases, where a sexual assault is suspected or obvious, the pathologist carries out his usual murder routine with special emphasis on certain aspects. These cases can be the most distressing of all to deal with, as all too often a small girl is the victim.

Strangulation or severe head injuries form the usual cause of death when accompanying sexual assaults. Some strangulations seem part of sexual gratification, and many instances have been recorded where a murderer was known to other prostitutes from his habit of partially throttling them during intercourse.

The cause of death in these cases is dealt with as in any other straightforward murder. Only in small children can the actual rape itself lead to death, from severe injuries and haemorrhage of the pelvic region.

Proof of a sexual assault on a dead body is arrived at in much the same way as the police surgeon proceeds in living victims. Apart from injuries to the genitals, there are frequently bruises, abrasions, finger-nail marks and even lacerations on the thighs and lower abdomen from frenzied attempts at opening the legs. One particular area is examined, especially in outdoor assaults — the prominences of the shoulder-blades and buttocks are commonly scratched or bruised, where the woman or girl has been forcibly pressed on to the ground. Leaves, earth or grass may help in confirming the circumstances.

The position of the clothing is naturally of great importance, though this is more the realm of the forensic scientist than the pathologist. Tears in clothing around the hips or breasts and especially stains are vital evidence to be pursued further in the laboratory.

The examination of the external genitals naturally forms a major part of the autopsy. Discoloration, bruising, tearing and swelling is noted, especially the apparent age of any such abnormalities. The findings will naturally bear a vastly different significance in a young virgin from an adult well used to intercourse. In the latter, it may well be impossible to say if recent coitus has occurred or not.

The presence of stains, whether from blood or seminal fluid is noted and swabs are taken for subsequent laboratory examination. These are obtained by using small wads of cotton-wool secured to the end of a thin stick or wire, the whole being protected for transport inside a test-tube. Samples are taken from the external genitals, the vaginal canal and the anus, even where no anal interference is suspected.

Motile spermatozoa may survive in the female genital tract for days and non-motile forms have been found more than two weeks later. After death, this period is much longer and in the Christie case of 1952, three of the victims had recognisable sperms in their vaginae, though death in one case was about three months earlier.

In the same year, one of the victims of Whiteway had been floating in the Thames for almost a week before discovery. The genital passages had been sealed with river algae and intact sperms were still recoverable at autopsy.

Internal examination of the pelvic organs is performed during the post-mortem, and the same search for recent injuries is made in the vagina.

Examination of the hymen is not as useful as might be expected, as in children, external injuries might give just as good information, and in older women the membrane is frequently absent. In older girls, who were virgin until the assault, then recent hymenal ruptures may be of assistance in confirming the occurrence of recent intercourse, but this, of course, is not the same thing as confirmation of forcible rape.

Other signs may be confirmatory of a sexual assault, such as bites on the face, neck or breasts. In some psychopathic sexual murders, not necessarily with a rape, gross mutilations may occur, as in the notorious Jack-the-Ripper killings of the last century and the Boston Strangler cases of very recent times. The Jack-the-Ripper phenomenon against prostitutes is not infrequently repeated, as in the recent series of West London stranglings.

All illegal sexual intercourse is by no means rape. The law dealing with such crimes has been consolidated in the 1956 and 1967 Sexual Offences Acts. A very brief resume of some of its definitions may clarify the somewhat complicated situation.

Rape is 'unlawful sexual intercourse with a woman by force against her will'.

'Force' includes not only sheer physical violence, but submission by fear, by fraud (such as impersonation of the husband) or by the use of drugs.

Fraud has consisted of things other than impersonation of the husband in the dark; in 1923 a singing teacher named Williams was charged with unlawful intercourse after persuading a young pupil that it would improve the quality of her voice. Several instances have been recorded of fraudulent persuasion that it was some form of medical treatment.

Doctors and dentists are particularly prone to false accusations of rape or indecent acts, as the administration of anaesthetics sometimes causes erotic hallucinations; a female chaperone is a vital necessity whenever a female patient is being anaesthetised; so far, there is no record of complaint from a man about a female practitioner!

A husband cannot be charged with the rape of his wife, though he could be convicted of inflicting bodily harm or assault.

Intercourse means any insertion, however slight, of the male organ within the woman's genital passage. Emission is not necessary, but unless some penetration takes place, the only charge that can be made is at most one of indecent assault.

The maximum penalty for rape is life imprisonment, emphasising that as a crime it is in the same class as murder and manslaughter. In some of the states of the U.S.A. it is a capital offence, at least in theory, since executions there have ceased for all practical purposes.

Rape is sexual connection without consent, at whatever age of the female; but even with full consent of the girl, intercourse is also a criminal offence in a variety of circumstances.

For a man to have sexual relations with a girl under 13 years of age is a serious crime, again punishable with a maximum of life imprisonment, even with her consent (which is held in law to be no consent at all due to her immaturity).

It is also an offence for a man to have intercourse with any girl under 16, but there is a special extenuating circumstance. If, in this age group of 13 to 16, the girl gave cause to appear more than that age (by dress, make-up and behaviour) and the man was under 24, with no previous similar convictions and he believed the girl to be over 16, he may be found not guilty. A similar provision excuses a man married (invalidly) to a girl under 16.

Intercourse with mental defectives is illegal at whatever age the woman might be, again because legally she is incapable of giving proper consent. Various degrees of family relationship, somewhat narrower than those decreed by the Church, constitute 'incest', making intercourse between these forbidden degrees an offence.

Another section of the Acts deals with 'unnatural offences', a rather prudish term for homosexual crimes. Under the original 1956 Act, all acts of 'buggery' (the lawyers appear to swing wildly from the prim 'acts of gross indecency' to the blunt Chaucerian Anglo-Saxon) were crimes serious enough to merit life imprisonment. This 'gross indecency' only applied to males; women, in spite of emancipation in other directions, are never mentioned in this form of legislation, which could send a man to prison for life.

However, in the 1967 Act it no longer became an offence for homosexual acts between consenting males in private. The age of consent is 21 and a public lavatory is specifically excluded from being a private place.

The examination of male bodies for signs of homosexual practices is occasionally required of the forensic pathologist. The significance of the 'bluebird' tattoo at the base of the thumb has been mentioned earlier as a recognition sign between homosexuals. The physical features of a long-term passive partner include dilation of the orifice and loss of the normal muscle corrugations with thickening of the skin at the margins.

Lesser sexual crimes include 'indecent assault', which ranges from mere interference with clothing to everything short of actual rape. These cases rarely concern the forensic pathologist, but form much of the difficult work of the police surgeon who volunteers to deal with such allegations.

Of much greater importance to the pathologist are the fatal complications of pregnancy. Of these, criminal abortion forms the major problem. Though there was a welcome spectacular fall in the deaths from abortion some years ago, when penicillin and other antibiotics were introduced, there are still a tragic number of deaths each year. It is too soon to see how the recent Abortion Act will affect these figures, but for a variety of reasons the criminal abortionist has by no means been put out of business by the limited legalisation for termination of pregnancy.

Prior to the Abortion Act of 1967, there was no legal justification for genuine medical termination of pregnancy, apart from an ambiguous mention in the Infant Life Preservation Act of 1929, which strictly refers to pregnancies later than twenty-eight weeks, which excluded the vast majority of therapeutic abortions.

To test the unsatisfactory state of the law in 1939, a well-known London gynaecologist openly performed an abortion on a 14-year-old girl, pregnant as the result of a multiple rape, on the grounds that her mental health would suffer if the pregnancy continued. He then invited a prosecution from the discomfited police; eventually the case came to trial, and, although the surgeon was acquitted, no change in the law was made for almost another thirty years.

The recent Abortion Act has been the cause of great controversy, with one section of the medical profession complaining that it is not wide enough in its provisions, and the other, together with a large body of religious and moral objectors condemning it for the opposite motives.

The main provisions of the Abortion Act are that it is now lawful for pregnancy to be terminated in certain approved institutions on certification by two doctors that it is justifiable because:

(i) continuation of the pregnancy would lead to a risk to life of the mother or injury to her physical or mental health or that of her existing family;

(ii) there is a substantial risk that the child would be born with such physical or mental abnormalities as to be seriously handicapped;

(iii) in coming to a decision about (i), the woman's actual or foreseeable environmental conditions may be taken into account.

Abortion means the premature termination of pregnancy at any stage during the nine months, though most take place within the first three or four months. A 'miscarriage' is another name for the same process and may come about either naturally or from deliberate interference.

It is impossible to discover the true incidence of abortion, but probably about one in five pregnancies abort, either naturally or otherwise. As long ago as 1939, it was estimated that there were about 150,000 a year. By the present time, this figure must have increased enormously, and probably almost half these are deliberately induced, mainly by the woman herself.

The law relating to all abortions (apart from those covered by the 1967 Abortion Act) is a very old one — more than a century old. It is the 'Offences Against the Person Act' of 1861, and deals with all sorts of physical violence. The relevant sections say that it is an offence for any person to procure or attempt to procure an abortion by the use of any 'instrument, poison or noxious thing'. This includes the woman herself, but *only* if she is in fact pregnant. If another person is involved, then it does not matter whether the woman is pregnant or not. Any person supplying drugs or instruments is also guilty of a lesser offence. A death arising as a result of a criminal abortion is regarded as manslaughter against the person performing the abortion. If a doctor is convicted of procuring a criminal abortion, he is automatically struck off the Medical Register.

Turning to the pathological aspects of criminal abortion, deaths can be caused by a variety of complications. In fact, considering the numerous hazards, it is remarkable that the death rate is so low.

The object of the exercise is to empty the womb of its unwelcome contents, which consist of the foetus (immature infant), its membranes, fluid and the placenta (afterbirth). The means employed to achieve this vary with the duration of the pregnancy and the experience and resources of the woman.

After the first missed period, there may be unease on the part of the woman, leading to fairly mild efforts 'just in case'. As the second month wears on and the second period is missed, then violent exercise, hot baths and all manner of drugs by mouth may be employed. The contents of the pregnant uterus are surprisingly tenacious, and where severe local violence has been employed to the abdomen, sufficient to cause death of the mother, the foetus has usually found to be quite intact. Thus these half-hearted measures rarely achieve success. Numerous herbal and other concoctions have been used to procure abortion. They were formerly sold openly in less reputable shops, and even now some thinly disguised 'Pills for Female Ills' may still be seen in odd corners.

Whatever drug is used, they have one thing in common — complete inefficiency! The amount of drug needed to cause abortion is almost the same as that to cause death in the mother, and this has happened on many occasions. There is no drug that acts specifically on the womb or its contents, and even hormones and drugs used in midwifery are virtually inactive at this early stage of pregnancy.

After the second and especially third period have been missed, more desperate measures are employed by the woman. These consist of mechanical means to interfere with the contents of the uterus. By far the most common, especially when performed by the woman herself, is the use of the Higginson syringe. Vaginal douching is useless and the only means with any hope of success is the introduction of fluid into the neck of the womb. *This is fraught with danger*, especially when done by the woman herself. The fluid, usually soapy water, has a froth upon it and in the emotion and discomfort of the procedure, the intake nozzle of the syringe can slip out of the fluid into the froth, thus pumping air bubbles under considerable pressure into the womb. This air can then find its way into the blood vessels of the pelvis and thence to the heart and brain, where it may cause rapid death. This process is called 'air embolism' and is a common fatal sequel to attempted abortion. The death may be immediate during the illegal 'operation' or may be delayed up to not more than about twenty minutes. Thus a woman who has had this done on the premises of a professional criminal abortionist may have time to leave the house and get some way towards home before death overtakes her; this information may be of use to police who are trying to locate a known professional.

The usual methods of the skilled professional abortionist, who regrettably is not infrequently a doctor or nurse, consist of the introduction of an instrument into the neck of the womb. Though sterile conditions may be used, and penicillin and other antibiotics be available, none of these procedures are free from risk. When the woman does them herself, the mortality is even higher.

The main risks are sudden death from 'vagal inhibition' — the reflex cardiac arrest described in the chapter on asphyxia; this can occur merely by touching the neck of the womb with the instrument, especially in a nervous, apprehensive woman. More often, direct injury takes place when the instrument is passed into the wrong part of the genital tract. This is again more likely to happen when the woman operates on herself. Severe haemorrhage or perforation of vital organs may be inflicted.

Sepsis is the ever-present fear; as mentioned, in years gone by this overshadowed all other factors and still occurs, again mainly with self-treatment, when the woman has no knowledge of sterilising instruments and no antibiotics available.

A particular type of sepsis is common, that of 'gas-gangrene' and the forensic pathologist may suspect this from the colour of the skin of the dead woman, which may be a peculiar bronze tint.

Of recent years, a singular method of attempted abortion has been seen in Britain — usually unsuccessful and potentially very dangerous. This is the application of certain commonly available crystals to the neck of the womb; the main interest lies in the fact that this is a method imported from America and most of the initial fatalities were associated with U.S. servicemen at bases in this country.

The pathologist's duties in examining fatal abortions are to arrive at the cause of death, to give his opinion as to whether it is likely to have been due to self-infliction or to outside interference and to offer any additional information from his experience, such as the crystal method mentioned above.

Where air embolism may have occurred from syringing, the brain and heart must be examined in a special way, so that the presence of air bubbles can be detected before they are lost during the post-mortem examination. Fluid from the vagina and uterus must be retained for analysis, as soaps and disinfectants may be identified and compared with substances found on the premises of suspect abortionists. The use of instruments is sought by searching for the marks of forceps on the neck of the womb — the presence of these strongly suggests the work of a medical abortionist.

Where death has occurred, it is the doctor's duty to give all the assistance he can to the investigating police, especially where it seems likely that professionals are implicated.

The reverse applies to family and hospital doctors, where no death or likelihood of death is present. Clinical doctors are under no obligation to notify abortions to the police (and the police have no particular desire to know!). As long ago as 1916 a medical professional organisation laid down the principles that a patient's condition is her own business, and if she does not wish her doctor to disclose this, he should not do so, unless ordered to do so by a court of law. Naturally, a fatal result alters this completely, and the doctor should at once report the case to the coroner.

Pregnancy can lead to quite natural complications causing death, including spontaneous abortion, kidney diseases, toxaemias and misplaced pregnancies outside the actual womb. These are fortunately very rare, considering the number of pregnancies in the community, but as death in women in the child-bearing age group is also very rare (they do not get the coronary artery diseases that kill men of the same age group), then a considerable proportion of the fatal deaths will be associated with pregnancy. This is so true that it is an axiom of pathologists that any woman dying in the childbearing age has suffered a complication of pregnancy until proved otherwise — and a great number of the 'otherwise' fraction will be found to have a haemorrhage into the membranes of the brain.

Though not a criminal offence, one type of fatality has a strong sexual element. These are the 'sexual asphyxias', briefly mentioned in the chapter on asphyxia. They were formerly and erroneously thought to be a strange form of suicide, and occasionally this verdict is returned by coroners unfamiliar with the condition.

The deceased is almost always a male, cases in females being so rare that they are discussed as curiosities at forensic conferences. The age group varies from the 'teens to the sixties, but the majority are young adults.

Allusions to the 'tip of the iceberg' are common these days, but it is never more true than when referring to these deaths, as the number of fatalities must represent an infinitesimal proportion of men who indulge in these peculiar practices. The circumstances are so typical that one glance at the scene or even a description over the telephone can settle the matter in the mind of any experienced forensic pathologist.

The essence of the condition is self-inflicted partial asphyxia, which induces perverse sexual exhilaration in these masochistically-inclined men. This is most frequently done by means of a noose around the neck, which can be tightened by some means under the control of the performer. Partial unconsciousness occurs, during which an orgasm takes place, then either voluntarily or by the limpness of the body due to the unconsciousness, the pressure is relaxed and the asphyxia passes off. This system is obviously a great potential danger, and when the mechanics of the device go wrong, the lapse into coma is unable to be reversed, and the victim is later found dead in these peculiar circumstances.

The strangulation apparatus is often a cord with a noose around the neck, the free end leading down the back to be tied to the ankles. By extending the legs, the noose can be tightened and pressure applied; when limpness supervenes from loss of consciousness, the cord relaxes and the pressure on the neck vanishes. This may work satisfactorily for months or years, but it only needs some kink in the cord or other slight upset to cause failure of loosening and then rapid death.

Other methods may be much more complicated, with pulleys and counterweights. Sometimes, a fixed noose may be rigged up and the man stands with his head inside it, producing pressure by leaning forwards. A case such as this would be difficult to distinguish from a suicide if it were not for the usual bizarre accompaniments at the scene. The man may be dressed in women's clothes, pornographic pictures may be within view and evidence of perversions such as masks, and rubber or plastic garments is common. Even more characteristic is the presence of bondage; apart from the asphyxiating cords, the wrists, ankles, waist and genitals may be lashed with rope, chains or even specially made fetters complete with padlocks. The presence of all these accoutrements is concrete evidence of the masochistic nature of the exercise, and death occurring during these procedures is an accident (or 'misadventure') and certainly not a suicide, as satisfaction and not self-destruction was the object of the victim.

Other methods are sometimes seen, apart from an asphyxiating ligature. Plastic bags may be put over the head to produce the perverse intoxication, anaesthetising substances may be sniffed such as plastic glues, cleaning fluid and many other organic chemicals. Masochistic exercises other than asphyxia are occasionally seen to have a fatal result — several cases of electrocution for 'thrills' have been reported, the fatality happening after many previous successful experiments, when some fault developed in the apparatus.

TEN — INFANTS AND CHILDREN

Sudden deaths in the young are particularly distressing whether due to crime, accident or natural causes. Most of the types of death that can happen to adults are seen from time to time in children, though some are thankfully rare in Britain. Murder in children is of a different pattern to adults. There are the sexual assaults, the fatal cases usually being strangulations.

Another kind of child murder never hits the headlines, though it inflates the 'murder' statistics. A mother — rarely a father, though it has happened — will commit suicide and take her children along with her, which then technically constitutes murder, often multiple. Mental disturbances, sometimes connected with recent childbirth, lead to this tragic situation — the woman may feel that the world is too bad for her children, or she may fear a nuclear war or merely feel utterly inadequate to bring them up properly. In any case, she kills them from love not hate, and the commonest method is for her to turn the gas on while they are asleep, killing herself at the same time.

Other types of murder are rare, such as stabbing or shooting. The 'battered baby', discussed fully later on, provides most examples of direct physical violence, but there are other problems peculiar to infants, namely the 'cot deaths' and deaths in the newly-born.

The first is dealt with later, and here the matter of infanticide is discussed.

Infanticide means exactly what the word implies, but in English law, it is sharply restricted to homicide during the first twelve months of life and only then if certain criteria are fulfilled — otherwise it is murder. Until the Infanticide Acts of 1922 and 1938, there was only a verdict of murder to cover such deaths. In years gone by, hundreds of distraught mothers must have been hanged — often on utterly erroneous medical evidence — for killing their infant children. For many years before the 1922 Act, juries had virtually refused to convict such unfortunate women. As acquittal seemed a poor answer to obvious guilt, the law was changed so that the harsh verdict of 'murder' could be changed to the lesser offence of 'infanticide', which now always carries a penalty of probation and psychiatric care.

The same legal manoeuvre was used in motor-car killings, where motorist juries, on the 'there-but-for-the-grace-of-God-go-I' principle, almost never found drivers guilty of manslaughter. The law was changed to bring causing death by dangerous driving within the ambit of the Road Traffic Act, with a maximum penalty of a few years prison or a heavy fine, rather than the possible maximum of 'life' for manslaughter.

Before this lesser charge of infanticide can be accepted, the action of the mother must be shown to have been caused by a "disturbance of reason caused by the effect of giving birth or by effect of lactation". As stated already, this can only hold good during the first year of the child's life and naturally the father cannot take advantage of the Act!

Having dealt with the law, the practical aspects are of frequent concern to the forensic pathologist. The bodies of newborn babies are brought to him with depressing regularity, this being almost a weekly occurrence in an area with a large population. The dead infants are found in all sorts of hiding places, as well as being left with no attempt at concealment. Plastic bags have become a common container, hidden beneath bushes, in streams, woods, derelict buildings and at the sides of roads. Where no real concealment has been attempted, they have been discovered in bedside lockers, beneath beds, in vanity-cases, chests of drawers and in attics. In most of these cases, unless the bodies have lain a long time undiscovered, there is often little trouble in tracing the mother; the opposite holds true for those discovered out-of-doors, as they have usually been deliberately dumped far from home.

Some dead infants are discovered immediately after the birth; the typical situation is the young unmarried girl, left alone in the house. The mother returns to find that her daughter has given birth in the bathroom or toilet and the baby is dead, either down the lavatory pan or with a severely marked neck. The exhausted, terrified girl often cannot honestly remember whether she deliberately harmed the baby or injured it in trying to deliver herself. Often in this sort of case, the elder woman maintains that she did not even suspect that her daughter was pregnant, let alone about to give birth!

The pathological problem in these cases is threefold: to estimate the age of the baby in months of maturity; to determine whether it was live or stillborn; and, if born alive, to discover the cause of death.

The duration of the pregnancy before birth is of importance because, in law, no foetus less than seven months (twenty-eight weeks) since conception is 'legally viable' — in other words, the law, from the point of view of any crime other than abortion, does not want to know about any baby less than seven months, as it legally does not exist. The law is occasionally confounded by six-and-a-half month babies that survive, but these have never yet been the subject of criminal proceedings!

If the child is more than seven months (determined as described in the chapter on identification by the presence of certain growth centres in the bones, size, weight and body features) then it must either have been live-born or stillborn.

The differentiation is extremely difficult and often impossible, especially in decomposed bodies.

The only definite sign of a stillbirth is 'maceration', which means a degeneration of the body tissues indicating death some time before whilst still in the womb. If ordinary post-mortem changes can be excluded, then this is cast-iron proof of stillbirth and no charge of murder or infanticide can lie.

In practice, the pathologist will say that all babies were stillborn unless he can display proof to the contrary. Negative evidence is no good, and the benefit of the doubt is always given to the mother — to the relief of the investigating police, who would have to make an often fruitless search for the mother, and when the luckless woman was found she would receive only sympathy and probation.

Proof of live birth in a child who may only have survived for a few minutes, is very intangible. The main criterion is the state of the lungs, as the main change at the time of birth is naturally the onset of breathing. Where respiration has been established for some hours, then it is fairly easy to say with confidence that the previously collapsed and airless lungs have been blown up and aerated. The difference in appearance is rather like that between a wet flannel and a bath sponge. Unfortunately for the pathologist, the survival time — if any — in most of the infants brought to him for examination, can be reckoned in minutes at most, and here the lung may show such minor changes as to make him reluctant to say that breathing has taken place. The older generations of pathologists, who usually wrote in a more confident vein on evidence that today is considered untenable, pinned complete faith in the ability of the lung that had breathed to float when dropped into water.

More recent critical tests have shown that, even when strictly controlled conditions are applied, this crude measure can often be wrong. One wonders how many women went to the gallows in the last century on the strength of this erroneous test — for in the early part of the nineteenth century, Britain was said to have more offences carrying the death penalty than any other country in Europe.

The flotation test may still be used as an adjunct to general examination, but the presence of the slightest degree of post-mortem decomposition invalidates even its tenuous indications; decay means gas formation, and this in itself will cause a lung to float. Microscopic examination of the lung may help in deciding whether the lung has been aerated, though again it is not as useful as one might expect. Infants who have been seen to breathe and then die have been examined and their lungs found to be apparently airless.

Another complication is the fact that the law defines a live birth as one where the baby has had a 'separate existence' from the mother. In royal disregard of any scientific sense, 'separate existence' is held to mean complete expulsion from the mother's body, excluding the umbilical cord and placenta (afterbirth). So a child breathing and yelling, but with one toe still inside its mother's birth passages, is *not* a separate person and cannot be the victim of murder or infanticide even if deliberately strangled in that situation! Neither is it an abortion, so until a law passed specially to bridge this gap was passed in 1929 (Infant Life Preservation Act), in theory, here was a loophole which allowed the possibility of deliberate homicide.

To prove that any breathing which may have occurred took place after the last toe had emerged from the mother, is almost impossible, unless late signs of delivery are found. These include drying of the umbilical cord, which happens after about a day and separation of the cord from the navel, which takes four or five days. Earlier proof is the presence of milk in the stomach, which is naturally incontrovertible evidence of existence for some time. As most of the dead infants die within minutes of birth, these later pieces of evidence are rarely forthcoming.

155

The causes of death in live births are numerous and again difficult to determine. Infanticide may be from *commission* or *omission*. Active violence includes strangling, suffocation, head injuries, stabbing and drowning. Injuries around the neck, mentioned earlier, may be due to the frenzied efforts of a lonely, inexperienced girl to hasten birth and not to deliberate acts designed to kill the child.

More often, death is due to acts of omission, due either to shock, ignorance or to deliberate attempts at causing death. The cord may not be cut, the air passages not cleared, or the child may be exposed to a low temperature.

The grip on life of a newborn baby is feeble enough at the best of times. With no medical care or even the assistance of a sympathetic mother, a lone woman can easily fail to give her new baby sufficient aid in the first few minutes to allow it to survive. Where no concrete evidence of deliberate killing can be found, then the pathologist usually gives the cause of death as 'inattention at birth', if definite signs are present that it was not a stillbirth.

ELEVEN — THE BATTERED CHILD

As Britain has one of the lowest murder rates in the world, even minor alterations in the pattern of murder become all the more apparent. Undoubtedly one of the most noticeable features of homicide in Britain in the last few years is the recognition of the 'battered baby' or 'battered child' syndrome. It is difficult to say whether the incidence has actually increased, or whether the apparent increase is due to recognition of cases which previously would have been called accidents — probably both factors exist together. In terms of criminal prosecutions for murder or manslaughter, the rise in cases of the battered baby is much less than the true incidence; due to the very nature of the crime, the majority are accompanied by insufficient evidence to allow the Director of Public Prosecutions to recommend even a charge being made, let alone the securing of a conviction.

The incidence is considerable, particularly in the United States. Kempe, in a twelve-month survey, collected 302 cases from seventy-one hospitals; thirty-three of these children died and eighty-five had permanent brain damage. Over the same period, he received reports of 447 cases from seventy-seven district attorneys; forty-five of these children died. There appears therefore, to be about a 10 per cent fatality rate, which agrees with estimates from other sources. Eleven states of the U.S.A. have now introduced legislation which obliges doctors to report to the authorities non-accidental injuries to children.

In probably no other type of homicide does medical evidence play such a big part, and in many of the cases the post-mortem findings may constitute almost all the available evidence. The importance of the doctor in these cases is appropriate, as doctors were responsible both for the lack of recognition of this syndrome for so many years, and for its eventual acceptance as true medico-legal entity. The story starts in 1946, when Caffey, an American radiologist, wrote a paper in an American medical journal, drawing attention to a series of cases in which there were curious limb fractures and brain membrane haemorrhages in young children. At that time, Caffey assumed these to be due to some disease process, but eleven years later he published a second paper in which he tentatively suggested that *injury* might be a better explanation than some hypothetical disease causing bone fragility. For several years some mild controversy was carried on in the medical press, but gradually more reports of these multiple fractures and subdural haemorrhages began to appear. Most of the interest was taken in the United States and Britain, and gradually it became obvious that injury to these children was, in fact, the *whole* basis of these multiple fractures. It took several more years for the idea to gain general acceptance amongst clinical doctors, and even today there are many physicians who are far from being sufficiently aware of the true nature of these cases. This is mainly due to the reluctance of doctors to believe that parents can deliberately inflict such severe and sometimes fatal injuries on their own small children; but during the last couple of years, publicity both in the medical and the lay press, has widened the appreciation of this so-called 'battered child syndrome'.

The pattern of child cruelty has undoubtedly changed over the last century. In the later years of the Industrial Revolution and well into the early part of this century, the classical type of ill-treatment of children was that of neglect, and it was for the alleviation of this type of case that the Child Protection Societies such as the N.S.P.C.C. were founded. Starvation, privation and general neglect have decreased in their more severe forms, due both to the efforts of these organisations and to the general increase in public awareness and social reforms. In its place, this new evil of 'baby battering' has appeared in a certain area of mankind. It seems limited to so-called 'civilised' communities; even within Western civilisation, the United States, Britain and, to a lesser extent, Germany and Scandinavia appear to be the only parts affected. In fairness, this may be a matter of reportage and availability of statistics, but there does seem to be a tendency for the Anglo-Saxon and Nordic races to be more inclined to ill-treat their children than the Latins, the Slavs and races further East.

Several surveys have been published in the United States, but in Britain the most active interest has been taken at the London Hospital by Professor Francis Camps and his colleagues. They recently published an analysis of their own cases in order to draw attention to various features of the syndrome. From this survey and from other published work, the following characteristics appear to emerge. The victims are usually very young, almost always under 2 years of age: of the fatal cases in London, more than half were less than one year old and more than three-quarters were under 2. All sorts of injuries may be present, but bruises and broken bones predominate. Fractured arms are common, as the immature bones around the joints are easily damaged by pulling, dragging and shaking of the baby's hands and wrists. Bruises of the cheeks, eyes and ears are often the result of the face being slapped or punched; blows to the head cause fractures and the internal bleeding that was one of the first features noticed in 1946. These head injuries are most often the actual cause of death in fatal cases, being next followed in frequency by damage to organs such as liver and intestines.

Bruising of the chest and abdomen and rupture of internal organs is not uncommonly found, and more bizarre violence occurs from time to time. Deliberate scalds, burning by electric fires, cigarette burns and even adult teeth marks have been seen.

One of the most characteristic findings in the dead babies is the presence of *old* injuries, indicating previous attacks on the infant. Healed fractures seen on X-ray (one of the characteristics of Caffey's early findings), old scars and fading bruises cry out for explanation: an illuminating quotation from the London Hospital report is that the "skin and bones tell a story which the child is too young or too frightened to tell".

As stated, the most characteristic feature is the presence of old injuries which have been inflicted on a previous occasion from the recent one which has led to the death. This is such a constant finding, that any baby found dead from an injury in circumstances which are in any way suspicious, must be completely X-rayed after death: the films may show up unexpected fractures in various stages of healing, which substantiate the suspicions of repeated violence on other occasions.

Another typical feature which adds to the circumstantial evidence is the delay in sending for medical help. In the London Hospital series there was an average interval of twenty hours between the injury and the seeking of a doctor's services. This no doubt is due to their realisation of guilt and consequent reluctance to call for assistance in the hope that the child will recover spontaneously.

For purpose of illustration, the following account might be taken as a typical example, having been compounded from several actual cases occurring in the last year or two.

A 23-year-old factory worker called the family doctor after midnight. On arrival the practitioner was shown a io-month-old female infant, lying dead in its carry-cot. On the left side of the head was an area of bruising, continued on to the ear.

On questioning the father and 21-year-old mother, the doctor was told that the father was bathing the child at seven o'clock that evening, and whilst being distracted by the two other older children, dropped the baby from his arms on to the edge of the galvanised bath, which stood in front of the fire. The child seemed all right at first, but later became pale, sick and drowsy. The doctor naturally declined to issue a death certificate and reported the case to the coroner. Next day, police questioning further discovered that the mother was out at 'Bingo' at the time, and that by now the father's story had slightly altered to the child falling on to the edge of the tiled hearth. Two months before, the same child was treated at a hospital casualty department for a fractured arm, allegedly sustained through falling from the settee.

Post-mortem examination revealed multiple fractures of the skull, situated in two separate areas of the head. Bruises of different ages were present on the child's chest, legs and arms. X-ray revealed a healing fracture of the right arm, a fracture of the collar bone of different date, two healed fractures of ribs and a swelling on the bone of the opposite arm (evidence of old injury).

When asked to explain these different injuries, the parents alleged that the other children were constantly knocking the younger child about, then later remembered several other incidents when the infant 'fell' against furniture. Further enquiries elicited the information that the husband had left the wife for some months before recently returning, and that he had alleged that he was not, in fact, the father of the dead child.

On being directly confronted with the medical opinion and accused by a senior detective officer of deliberately injuring the child, he made a voluntary statement admitting that he had given the infant several heavy slaps and punches to "stop it yelling" when he was putting the children to bed; he further admitted slapping the child on other occasions, but denied any more violent abuse. He said that the previous fracture and falls had always occurred when the child was in the care of the mother.

Both were charged with manslaughter, the father being given twelve months imprisonment, and the mother placed on probation.

These features, pathetic and sometimes sickening though they may be, are fairly easy to understand. What is much more difficult to evaluate is the social and psychological background which leads to their infliction. The 'battered babies' are a different class altogether from the dirty, half-starved victims of classical child neglect. They are usually well nourished and well dressed, coming from at least average homes, though no social class is exempt. In Professor Camps' series, they tended to come from the 'working class' though a medical student and State-registered nurse were included amongst the parents. Reports from the United States claim a higher proportion of unstable, immoral, alcoholic or feeble-minded parents, but in Britain no such definite features can be found in the majority of the offenders. Some of the parents seem to have some personality defect — domestic discords are common and the mother may tend to be a weak, ineffectual type with an aggressive, intolerant husband. Obviously, considerable research is needed into the mental make-up of the parents to discover any significant factors of this nature. The father tends to be accused more often than the mother of causing the child's injuries or death: in the London Hospital series in these cases which led to prosecutions, 34 per cent involved the father and 21 per cent the mother. There is a tendency for the police and judiciary to be biased against the male parent where a choice has to be made, but some of the most appalling injuries have in fact been admitted to by the mother.

A high 'suspicion index' is required in doctors who deal with children, but, from the very nature of their vocation, this attitude is often lacking. Kempe states that the 'battered child syndrome' should be always considered by clinicians in any child exhibiting fracture of any bone, subdural haematoma (bleeding beneath the skull), failure to thrive, soft tissue swelling, skin bruising or where the degree or type of injury is at variance with the history given.

The child is almost always the youngest in the family, and an alternative name for the condition might be the 'Cinderella syndrome'. In a family of two or three children, it is common to find that the elder children are never physically harmed, but the youngest appears to act as a scapegoat for the others. One mother even admitted that when the elder children were chastised by the father, she could not bear to see the younger one 'getting away with it' and would promptly set about it to even up the score. The younger victim may often be the subject of marital dispute in that it may be illegitimate, or the father may suspect it to be so. Again it may be unwanted, and in fact may be a failure of contraception or even attempted abortion. This attitude of rejection may be an extremely important causative factor in the syndrome, and is of interest not only to paediatricians, but to those doctors and social workers whose interest lies in family planning and the termination of pregnancy.

The difficulties of dealing with this syndrome are great, both from the point of view of punishment and prevention.

Actual detection — which until a few years ago was virtually nil — is somewhat better these days, thanks to the more enlightened attitudes and education of doctors, and to a certain extent of the lay public, who are encouraged to report to the N.S.P.C.C. or other authorities any cases of ill-treatment. However, as this is almost entirely a domestic crime, witnesses are almost always absent. The parents often show considerable ingenuity in avoiding notice being drawn to the repeated injuries to the children. The child may be taken to a different doctor on each occasion, and even to a different hospital casualty department. The parents, especially the father, are characteristically able to provide a glib explanation, and as far as each individual event is concerned this explanation is often quite acceptable. It is only when a sequence of similar events is discovered that explanations become less plausible, hence the imperative need for X-raying to determine the presence of earlier injuries, as well as a most careful investigation into the history of the case.

It has been estimated that a child suffering a first injury in this way has a 60 per cent chance of returning on subsequent occasions with further injuries, and a io per cent chance of eventually receiving a fatal injury.

Until more is known about the psychiatric make-up of the parents, it seems unlikely that any preventative measures can be taken. Usually one can only be wise after the event. Punitive measures against the parents, even when evidence is available, is really of very limited value. It can do the dead child no good, and often the other children in the family are in no similar danger. Certainly the fear of punishment can be of little use as a deterrent, as these acts are often committed in moments of emotional stress or even frenzy. It is common knowledge that most children can drive even the most sane and respectable parent to the brink of some violence, but in the majority of cases there is sufficient self-control for acts of savagery to be avoided and certainly not to be repeated.

Unfortunately, there is a significant number of parents in the community with insufficient self-control. Whether due to marginal mental defectiveness, psychological abnormalities or less definable characteristics, the end result is the same — the battered child. Until such ill-defined root causes are clearly understood and somehow made amenable to treatment, the only weapons available are constant awareness and suspicion amongst clinicians and pathologists; understanding of the syndrome amongst policemen, lawyers and the judiciary; and willingness of the general public to report any suspicion of child cruelty to the authorities. The last is extremely important and cases of obvious gross ill-treatment have in the past been ignored by neighbours. This is not due to sheer callousness, but to a fear of 'getting involved' and perhaps a fear of arousing unwarranted suspicions — yet the N.S.P.C.C. and Children's Officers are most discreet in their enquiries. With more education of the lay public in this matter, more widespread reportage of cases could reduce at least the repetitive cruelty and all-too-frequent deaths. The main object is the removal of the child from danger rather than the punishment of the offenders.

TWELVE — SUDDEN DEATH IN INFANCY

One of the most important functions of the forensic pathologist is not only to examine and interpret deaths from obvious criminal causes, but to exclude natural deaths from accidents, suicides and murders. This function of exclusion can save police forces and other investigators much unnecessary work and expense; errors in this 'filtration system' have led in the past to several frustrating and abortive murder hunts where no murder was ever committed.

The matter of sudden unexpected death in infants is related to this function of exclusion. Though the scientific investigation of homicide figures largely in the popular mental image of forensic pathology, the most pressing research problem in the forensic world today is the mystery of sudden infant deaths, and, both from a medical research point of view and the amount of personal and social disturbance which it causes, some appreciation of the problem should be made by all those connected with law enforcement.

The sudden unexpected death in infants (now universally becoming known as 'SUD') is a natural phenomenon but one of such an obscure nature that it is all too frequently confused with deaths from accidents, manslaughter from negligence, or sometimes even wilful homicide. The magnitude of the problem is far greater than many realise, and unfortunately, many more do not realise that any problem exists at all! Due to the sudden nature of the fatality, with little or no previous illness, clinical medical practitioners have almost no contact with SUD. The pathologist is often the only doctor to have any extensive experience of the condition, and thus the whole orbit of interest is somewhat circumscribed. Returning to the actual numbers, at least 1,500 children in England and Wales die each year in this obscure manner, and it is clear that this is a gross underestimate, the total numbers probably being in the region of 3,000 to 5,000 deaths. In the United States about 15,000 cases occur, and a most reputable paediatric authority suggests that 25,000 is a more realistic figure. This represents about a quarter of all infant deaths from all causes, and far exceeds deaths from polio or road accidents in the infant age group. In Britain, even taking the relatively conservative figure of 3,000 deaths per year, this represents a massive problem, when it is considered that the cause of death is quite unknown. Imagine public outcry if 3,000 infants died from some known preventable disease or from traffic accidents! One only has to remember the recent public and press furore when relatively minor outbreaks of gastro-enteritis caused a few infant deaths in hospitals.

Before discussing the many problems surrounding the SUD syndrome, a clear picture of what it means must be offered. Basically, a 'sudden unexplained infant death' concerns a young child, usually from two to six months of age, who was either quite well or had only trivial symptoms, who is found dead in bed, almost invariably in the morning. This circumstance is so constant that the alternative name to SUD is 'cot death', or in America 'crib death'.

This tragic thumb-nail sketch must be elaborated to fill in details. The age range within which SUD occurs may be anything from two weeks to two years. It is thus *not* a condition of newborn children, and death in the first couple of weeks of life excludes cases from this mysterious condition. This range of two weeks to two years is rather wide, and the great majority of children die between two months and six months with a peak at four months.

The sex of the children does not seem a vital factor, but in most surveys, boys outnumber girls in the ratio of about three to two. Other surveys have shown a preponderance of girls, but the general opinion is that males are affected most, though it is apparent that sex differences play little or no part in the basic cause.

A vitally important feature, which must be somehow related to the cause, is the *seasonal* variation in SUD. Sudden death in infancy is virtually confined to the cold wet months, and in Britain almost all cot deaths occur between October and May, with a peak in December and sometimes a smaller peak in the early spring. The peaks do not seem related to weather temperatures, nor to any discernible variation in climate from week to week. One of the many theories of cot deaths was that hypothermia (low body temperature) was a factor, but this is not borne out by the facts. These months, however, are significant for one very good reason — these are the months of widespread respiratory infections, colds, coughs and general increase in throat and lung infections. As will be mentioned later, this seems the most likely causative factor in an otherwise occult disease pattern.

The social status of the families in which SUD occurs is again rather debatable. It is certainly numerically true that the children of the lower income groups suffer more heavily, but this may be less significant than is first apparent. Firstly, there tend to be more children in the families of the lower income groups, and they live in smaller houses, thus there is much more opportunity for cross infection, if respiratory disease is held to be the cause. Another factor which must be taken into account, though it is probably much less important than the first, is that deaths in the upper groups of the Registrar-General's social classification are less likely to be reported to the coroner than are those of the lower income groups. This phenomenon exists in adult deaths as well as children, there being a tendency for sudden natural deaths in upper-class districts, especially among private patients, to be reported less than in the rest of the community.

Factors such as premature births, illegitimacy, etc. have at various times been reported to be different in the SUD children than in the normal population pattern, but this appears to have little bearing on the background of the syndrome.

Very often a retrospective history of a case shows that the child will have had a cold or 'snuffles' or some slight bowel upset in the days preceding the death. Even this factor is slightly suspect, as naturally no *prospective* research can be carried out, only a back-ward-looking investigation after the death has occurred. In these circumstances, the bereaved and anguished parents will search, perhaps subconsciously, for some rational explanation for the death, and possibly one which may relieve them of real, if unfounded, feelings of guilt. Therefore trifling disorders such as colds and diarrhoea will be remembered, though in fact it is possible that the incidence of these is no greater than in other children, especially in these winter months when minor infections are almost universal. In many cases, even this trifling history is lacking, and the child had been quite well up to the time of being found dead.

Death almost always occurs in the sleeping place, and almost always when the child is asleep. This history of being put to bed in normal health, and either being found dead in the early morning, or having been found well at a 6 a.m. feed, then placed back in the cot and being found dead later in the morning, is so constant that one might almost have a rubber stamp for the history. A child found dead in the afternoon or evening more often shows some condition which makes it *not* a true cot death, and certainly all such cases where death has not occurred in the early morning must be treated with even more attention to detail than the others. Even so, some of these show no cause of death whatsoever and there is no alternative but to classify them with the main group, which are always found dead in the morning.

From this point the problem takes two main directions, one purely medical and the other partly medico-legal and partly social.

The medical scientific aspect concerns the underlying pathology which causes the condition, and as yet almost nothing can be said with certainty. SUD has been known literally for thousands of years, but little progress has been made during that time. In the Old Testament, when Solomon was called upon to arbitrate between two women's claims to a baby, the woman who had lost her own baby was probably the first recorded mother of an SUD. Since then, especially in the past fifty years, innumerable statistical surveys and research investigations have been carried out. Time after time theories have been put forward only to be demolished within a very short space of time. This is not the place to go into detailed account of the various speculations, but a couple of the more outstanding must be mentioned. That of an overwhelming virus infection leads the field, though it has never been proven. The protagonists say that the age group in which the children die, usually two to six months, is the time when natural immunity passed via the placenta from the mother has been exhausted, and yet the child has not had the opportunity to develop its own. Therefore in this period, the child is very vulnerable to virus infections of all types, which may not be lethal to older babies. Unfortunately, no reduction in the fraction of the blood proteins which contain immune antibodies can be demonstrated in SUD cases, nor has any significant recovery of viruses been attained from the autopsies on these children.

About nine years ago, British researchers discovered that almost all bottle-fed babies had antibodies to cow's milk in their blood. It was found that animals who were made sensitive to cow's milk and then were given tiny quantities of milk protein down their windpipes, whilst under barbiturate anaesthesia to simulate the sleep of the baby, died instantly from an allergic reaction. It was further found that the SUD cases tended to have higher quantities than control children. This was a very attractive theory, but has not stood the test of time, mainly because the antibodies to cow's milk appear within days of birth, whereas death is usually around the four-month mark. Other theories include the inability of the child to breathe through the mouth where the nose is blocked by either catarrh or a cold, spinal haemorrhages in the neck region, abnormalities in calcium levels in the blood due to glandular defects, and many other theories which have not been confirmed by further work. From the medical point of view we just do not know. Mainly from the marked seasonal incidence, it seems most likely that some non-specific virus infection of the air passages and lungs may be responsible, but as yet this cannot be proved.

At post-mortem examination almost nothing is found, and if anything significant is found, then by definition the death does *not* belong to the SUD group. Occasionally, true bronchopneumonias are found, and this at once gives a satisfactory explanation for the death. But in the vast majority of cases where this history exists, the only thing that is found are small haemorrhages on the surface of the lungs and heart. These small haemorrhages, called petechiae or 'Tardieu's spots' have unfortunately raised a large red-herring in the SUD syndrome. They are classically found in deaths from asphyxia and were previously regarded as the inevitable hallmark of suffocation or strangulation. From this association it was erroneously thought for many years that SUD must be the result of asphyxia, and from this much confusion and social distress has arisen.

In the earlier part of this century, before SUD was recognised as such, sudden infant deaths were called 'over-laying', and this term has persisted to the present day, with many unfortunate results. 'Over-laying' meant Ae smothering of a child sharing the same bed as an adult, and was thought to occur because the children, who in former days slept far more in the family bed than in separate cots, were found dead in the morning — often with their face in the pillow or mattress, and with the body of the adult either on top of, or very near the child. The fact that scores of millions of children have spent their entire infancy and childhood in their parents' bed and survived without trouble, has not prevented the survival of this concept of sudden infant death. It wras further consolidated by the presence of the small haemorrhages, which were taken as a Gospel sign of asphyxia. Today, there are still many pathologists and coroners willing to believe that over-laying is a valid occurrence, but in fact it has no scientific foundation. In passing, it might be mentioned that Section I of the Children's and Young Person's Act of 1933 made it a criminal offence for any intoxicated adult to have shared a bed with an infant less than 3 years old where the death of that infant was caused by suffocation. This section is indexed in Stone's *Justice's Manual* under 'over-laying' and is an example of a piece of legislation enacted for a condition which probably never existed!

Another red-herring was the presence of vomit in the air passages as the cause of death. It is very commonly found in post-mortem examinations of all types, especially in children who often have a stomach filled with milk curds. Many doctors record 'aspiration of vomit' as the cause of death, whereas in fact this is an agonal phenomenon related to the 'death rattle' and is an *effect* of death, not a *cause* of death. This, coupled with the presence of the spurious 'asphyxia' haemorrhages on the surface of the lungs, has led to many thousands of babies being labelled as 'suffocation from regurgitation of vomit', and thus an inquest was usually held, when in fact the death was due to entirely natural, if obscure causes.

The social aspects of this distressing condition mainly affect the parents. Feelings of open guilt at neglecting some trivial symptoms like a cold are added to their natural bereavement, and the addition of the extra psychological trauma of an open inquest and possibly the scathing and unfriendly comments of an unenlightened coroner are sometimes too much to be borne. Certainly mental breakdowns have occurred, especially in the mothers, and one suicide can almost certainly be laid at the door of such unnecessary public inquisition in such a case. Apart from feelings of self-reproach, occasionally the feelings are directed against other persons. Sometimes the baby is left in the care of relatives or friends, and if a cot death occurs under these circumstances, there may be open conflict between the parents and the custodian, or permanent smouldering feelings of antagonism which may lead to family friction. The same open or implied blame may lie between mother and father.

Furthermore, the family doctor may suffer; many times the parents have questioned or openly expressed dissatisfaction with the standard of care of the doctor, and occasionally florid accusations of negligence have occurred. In one recent inquest, the doctor's face was slapped in public by a distraught mother. All this arises from completely false premises, as the death really was from natural causes, quite unpreventable in the present state of medical knowledge!

One cause of this unhappy situation could be remedied by a relatively simple administrative change. As the condition of 'sudden death in infancy' is not recognised in official statistics, it cannot be given as an acceptable cause of death on a death certificate or post-mortem report. The legal fiction of some natural cause such as 'acute bronchiolitis', 'acute tracheobronchitis' or 'capillary bronchitis' is frequently used to avoid the inquest, but these are quite without scientific foundation. Thus no means of retrieving accurate statistics on cot deaths are available, and also the statistics of the true respiratory diseases are falsely inflated by these additions.

A new category, called by any name that is readily recognisable, would solve these problems and also solve another more immediate problem, that is the bewilderment of the parents on reading such a cause of death. Even without medical knowledge, 'acute bronchiolitis' is near enough to 'acute bronchitis' to suggest to the parents that death was due to an infection of the lungs. They then feel that they must have neglected the previous symptoms, or that relatives neglected them, or that the family doctor was ignorant and negligent in neglecting them. Again all this turmoil is quite unnecessary, as acute bronchiolitis is nowhere near the real cause of death. A simple reform of the Registrar-General's categories is urgently needed to correct this state of affairs.

When this argument has been put forward it has been countered that this might hide criminal or unnatural causes of death. This, of course, is not so. At every autopsy, child or otherwise, the pathologist starts with an open mind and, depending on what he finds, the ultimate decision can go in any direction. In SUD, by definition, no significant pathology is exposed, and the real cause of death is quite obscure (though it fits in with this well-known pre-determined pattern): it is only then that the pathologist is in need of a special term to embrace the 'sudden death in infancy' syndrome. Any other finding indicating violence, poison or any other unnatural cause would prevent him ever getting to a point where he needed to use this special term, and thus the objections of those who think that criminal actions might be blanketed by the free use of a new term are unjustified. Some pathologists think that as the classical features of asphyxia, namely small haemorrhages in the lungs etc., are usually present, one cannot tell that the child has *not* been suffocated, and therefore a public inquest is necessary. This view is also entirely unjustified. Firstly, the signs of asphyxia are not necessarily accompanied by petechial haemorrhages, especially in children. Secondly, no one would sensibly allege that about 3,000 children in Britain are murdered by suffocation every year! Thirdly, a public inquest is not going to unearth any more facts than those discovered by the coroner's officer or police officer in his preliminary enquiry. No witnesses are present at the death, and if the parent is going to confess to murder, he or she will do so, inquest notwithstanding. In any case, not one atom of evidence has ever been forwarded in this condition to suggest that homicide is a factor worth considering seriously. In fact, the opposite occasionally occurs; in several cases of apparent cot death, the mother has gone to the police at a later date and confessed to smothering the child. In almost all the cases recorded, this confession is quite untrue, there being a hysterical-psychiatric condition which has forced the mother to confess to the murder of her child from some obscure and deep-seated effects of the neglect-guilt feelings.

These oddities are off the main stream of the syndrome. Sudden death in infancy is a major problem in world medicine, and certainly the most pressing problem in the field of forensic pathology, though it by no means gets the limelight which it deserves. In the United States there are now many groups of people across the country, with a national federation, which devote themselves to supporting medical research and dissemination of information on the subject. The members of these Guilds for Infant Survival are mostly parents who have themselves suffered cot deaths, and have banded together to raise money and enthusiasm for investigating the problem. They contact recently-bereaved parents in order to comfort them and relieve them of the bewilderment and self-reproach which surrounds the condition, and organise seminars and provide research money for medical workers. From the purely humanitarian aspect of giving support to newly-bereaved parents, this system is very worthwhile, and a similar guild in Britain would be a significant advance towards removing the obscurity which surrounds the condition. Perhaps the most pressing needs are for a new category for registering the cause of death, and the enlightenment of every coroner and coroner's pathologist into the completely natural basis of SUD.

THIRTEEN — STAINS, SERUM AND SCIENCE

Once more we find a section of forensic medicine which originated with the 'jack of all trades' pathologists of past decades, but has been passed over to scientific specialists, due to rapidly increasing complexity of techniques.

The examination of blood and other biological fluids, whether as fluids or stains, is now dealt with either by the Home Office laboratories or by sub-sections of the few larger university departments of forensic pathology.

Stains are of prime interest to the forensic scientist, and at scenes of crime his eyes are always on the lookout for any suspicious smears on the clothing or surrounding furniture, floor or fabrics. Bloodstains are the most common in violent crimes, though seminal stains, sweat, urine and saliva can be important.

When a stain is detected, the first thing to establish is whether it is blood or not. Many things are brown or red and, especially when absorbed on to cloth or some other absorbent surface, they can mimic blood quite well. Suspect stains on a hard surface may be scraped off into a small tube, but only after they have been photographed and examined, as the position and shape may be of some help. A star-shaped blood splash has probably hit the surface perpendicularly, whilst an oblique impact will leave a narrow ellipse, often with a separate globule at the front end like an exclamation mark, to indicate the direction of travel.

Establishing the fact that it is blood is fairly easy, as a range of tests exist to do this. The simpler ones, such as the benzidine test, or phenolphthalein test may give a positive reaction with fruit or vegetable juice, puss, rust and many other contaminants, though a strong rapid positive result is good presumptive indication of blood. The test depends on the presence of an enzyme 'peroxidase', which is present in blood, but also in many other biological extracts.

On clothing or other surfaces where no destructive testing can be performed, the reaction is so sensitive that all that needs to be done is to press a damp filter paper on the surface and then conduct the test on the paper — sufficient of the stain will be removed to allow the colour reaction to occur. This can be useful for screening large areas of fabric; big sheets of damped paper are laid on, then removed and sprayed with the reagents, so that a 'map' of any positive areas is obtained and their relationships established. This method is particularly useful when searching for seminal stains.

Where this preliminary peroxidase screening is positive, the stains can be confirmed as being due to blood in several ways. A minute amount may be dissolved and looked at through a spectroscope, when the characteristic absorptions bands of haemoglobin will be evident. There are several other chemical tests which display the presence of this red pigment from the blood cells.

The age of a bloodstain is hard to estimate, but experienced scientists in the forensic laboratories can often separate the very fresh from the not-so-fresh and from the definitely 'ancient'. In dried stains, the cells are usually all destroyed and microscopic confirmation is not possible; neither is the sexing of the blood by examination for the Barr body of the female nucleus; occasionally, menstrual blood may be recognised by the presence of large cell remnants from the interior of the womb, though a more reliable technique has recently been developed, in which a special protein which prevents menstrual blood from clotting, is detected by 'electrophoresis'.

Having confirmed a stain as blood, the next problem is to discover whether it is human or animal. This always has to be proved in criminal cases, in case the accused alleges that the blood on his sleeve dripped off his Sunday joint as he was putting it in the oven! Identification of species other than human may also be important in non-murder cases such as theft of carcases, sheep-worrying by dogs and the not infrequent finding of bloodstains on vehicles or railway engines, where no one knows what has been hit.

Species identification is established by the use of specific antisera. Every type of animal has its own blood-protein pattern and reacts strongly to the introduction of any foreign protein from another, by producing a neutralising substance specific for the foreign protein, called 'anti-body'. The whole process is called 'immunisation' and the study of such serum reactions is 'immunology', a subject which is now vast and expanding almost explosively.

If a rabbit is injected with a minute quantity of dog's blood, it will produce an 'anti-dog' antibody. If a second injection is given, there might be a violent reaction which might even kill the rabbit — this is one of the dangers of incorrect blood transfusion in man. If the rabbit's 'anti-dog' serum is mixed in a test tube with dog serum, a visible reaction occurs, a cloudy ring appearing at the junction of the two fluids. A more sophisticated method is to allow them to diffuse towards each other in a small film of gelatine when a cloudy zone will appear at the mixing point.

Anti-sera can be made against any animal and against human blood. In testing our suspect stain, it is soaked so that some of the protein is dissolved. This fluid is then tested against anti-human serum from a rabbit. A positive reaction is proof of a human origin; if negative, the whole range of animal sera are tried until a match is made.

This is an oversimplification of the technique which is called the 'precipitin test'. Control tests have to be run on the unstained part of the fabric etc., to make sure that no interfering substance in the cloth is causing a false reaction. Other methods of species identification have recently been developed, but these complex techniques are the realm of the immunologist.

Now that we have the presence of human blood confirmed, the last step is to determine the blood *group*. This again is an enormous science in its own right, both from the blood transfusion aspect and the genetic and serological aspects, many of which have medicolegal significance. In cases of violent crime, whether assaults or homicide, it may be of the utmost importance to match blood found either on a weapon, at a scene, on the body or on the clothing of the victim, with blood from another source.

For example, blood found on the clothing of a strangled woman — who had no source of bleeding to account for it — may have been caused by her successfully scratching her assailant. If a suspect is charged, confirmation that this bloodstain was of identical group to his and quite different from that of the victim, would add to the circumstantial evidence of his presence at the scene, though it could not, at the present state of scientific knowledge, *prove* that he was involved, as would a fingerprint.

Similarly, blood found on a weapon discovered in the possession of a suspect might be of identical group to that of a stabbed victim, and again would help to add to the weight of evidence against him.

Bloodstains or fragments of skin beneath the fingernails of a murdered person may also be blood-grouped (as skin, in common with all body cells, shares the same blood-group characteristics). This technique again would provide strong supplementary evidence of a 'contact trace' between the accused and the victim.

The blood-group systems are numerous and becoming more complex each year, as further sub-divisions are discovered. In addition to actual blood groups, which are a function of the red blood cells, there are similar inherited characteristics in the serum, the fluid part of the blood, which have become useful adjuncts to the grouping techniques. These include different types of haemoglobin, haptoglobins and an enzyme (choline esterase), all of which need special apparatus for their detection.

Using all these factors, blood can be sub-divided into hundreds of permutations, every person's particular permutation being fixed for life and determined by heredity. The more new factors that are discovered and applied to the tests, the more specific the blood pattern of a person can be determined. We have not yet reached the point where a positive identification can be made, but on grounds of statistical significance, very short odds can sometimes be given on two identical, detailed patterns having come from the same person or identical twins. Unfortunately for the forensic scientist, this high degree of accuracy can only be achieved on fresh liquid blood samples, and in crime one of the samples will almost invariably be a dried stain, which cannot be used for many of the more exotic grouping techniques. However, continuing advances in technology are constantly pushing back the boundaries of these disadvantages.

The actual blood groups involved are the main ABO groups, so-called because red cells contain either A substance (Group A blood), B substance (Group B blood), both substances (Group AB blood) or neither (Group O). There are further subdivisions of these groups, but the next separate system is the Rhesus group, well known for its occasional troubles in newborn babies. This system is not amenable to testing in dried stains, and another set, the MN group, is employed forensically when dealing with non-liquid samples. Many other systems exist, such as

Kell, Duffy, Lutheran etc., but, apart from paternity cases where liquid samples are available, these cannot be used. The non-red cell constituents like various haemoglobins and haptoglobins have more recently come into routine use in the criminal aspects of serology.

Grouping is of considerable use in criminal cases with body fluids other than blood, mainly saliva and semen. The examination of suspected seminal stains forms a considerable part of the work of the biological department of a forensic laboratory. Before grouping can be performed, suspect stains must be positively confirmed as being seminal, as in the case of blood. Formerly this was a very laborious task, involving extraction of the stain into solution and then attempting to form various specific crystals by chemical means. As many suspect stains were not seminal at all, this was a long process and in the last few years, a screening technique has considerably speeded up the task. The usual objects to be tested are female underclothes, though any clothing or bed-clothes etc. may be under suspicion. The fabric is covered by large sheets of damp blotting paper, which soak up minute amounts of the stains. They are then sprayed with chemicals from an aerosol gun, which will develop a bright purple colour if the enzyme 'phosphatase' is present. This enzyme is contained in large amounts in semen, originating in the prostate gland. As with the benzidine test for blood, a 'map' of positive spots can then be obtained on the large paper sheets and the point of origin on the clothing detected. As the test is not specific for semen — though almost so — these highly suspect areas are further examined. The fabric fibres are tested out in fluid and examined microscopically for spermatozoa. This can be a long ob and considerable experience is needed to recognise the sperms after distortion by drying on the cloth. A more recent method of confirmation is by the use of an 'anti-semen' immunological test, similar to that described for species identification.

Once positively identified as semen, the stain may then be dissolved and tested for its blood group, in much the same way as for bloodstains, though a snag is that 20 per cent of people do not secrete their blood group substances in fluids like semen or saliva.

The mention of saliva brings to notice the fact that even the minute trace on a cigarette stub may be enough to establish the blood group in the 80 per cent who are 'secretors'. Nasal mucus and sweat also have group characteristics, and stains from suffocating pillows etc. may be tested to confirm that these have been in close contact w ith a person of the same blood group, though of course, in common with all other cases, this cannot be taken to mean that it was the identical person.

The other great use of blood-group evidence in legal medicine is not in connection with crime, but with civil litigation concerned with divorce and parenthood.

Where one party to divorce proceedings alleges that adultery has taken place because the child cannot be his, he may call scientific evidence to show that the particular combination of blood groups amongst himself, the wife and the child is incompatible with his being the father.

Far more often, the dispute is between an unmarried mother who alleges that a certain man is the father of her child and that he should contribute towards its maintenance. If the man (called the 'putative father' until proved otherwise) denies the allegation, then the only way of getting nearer the truth is by blood grouping of all the parties involved. It sometimes happens that a woman may have a choice of several 'putative' fathers, and again grouping may be the only way of clearing up the confusion.

The courts have come to rely heavily on blood-group evidence, but British law has not yet made such testing obligatory, as in some continental countries. Yet refusal of a party to allow a blood test is taken notice of when coming to a decision. Blood grouping can never positively *identify* the father, but can definitely *exclude* him. Like the stains in criminal work, the more research progresses, the better the statistical evidence becomes towards pointing the finger at any one man. In this work, there is one great advantage — that of having fresh liquid blood samples, which considerably extends the range of groups and other blood constituents that can be tested.

The complexities of blood grouping in disputed paternity are great, but a simple example using ABO, the commonest group system, will serve as an illustration.

A mother (Group A) alleges that Mr. Smith is the father of her child (Group AB). He denies it and submits to a blood test as well. (In practice, they are usually all tested at the same time. All three attend a doctor for small quantities of blood to be taken either by syringe or a needle-prick. They must identify themselves in the presence of each other, or of a solicitor, to the doctor, so that there can be no substitution or mix-up.)

When the results are examined it is seen that Mr. Smith is Group A, like the mother. This at once excludes him from being the father, as the child has a B in its blood cells and this could not have got there either from the mother or the putative father, Mr. Smith. Some other man must be responsible, being of blood group B or AB.

If Mr. Smith had been Group B, this would by no means have indicated that he *was* the father, only that he *could* have been. This will be taken into account when considering all the other nonmedical aspects of the case, such as time of access to the woman, the nature of their relationship, the physical appearance of the child, etc.

The relative narrowness of the 'possibility bracket' is important in coming to a decision. If a man was of the right group to be the possible father, then if this was Group O, no less than 47 per cent of the population would be in the same position! Group A show 42 per cent and Mr. Smith's Group B (in the second instance above) drops sharply to only 8 per cent, so a magistrate or judge would be more influenced by probabilities if he was a B rather than the wide open O or A.

With Group AB, the bracket narrows even further to 3 per cent, but when compared with modern techniques of multiple Rhesus, MNS, the ABO exclusion is really crude. With the addition of other serum constituents mentioned earlier, exclusion of paternity can be attained in almost three-quarters of innocent men.

On the other hand, certain rare combinations of groups can prove that, for example, only one in 40,000 men could have produced the child that was alleged to have been conceived by the accused. Even here, though the judges will be strongly influenced by the medical evidence, it cannot be taken as absolute *proof of* paternity, and the role of grouping still remains primarily an exclusory test.

FOURTEEN — POISONING

In probably no other field of forensic medicine has the climate changed so much as in toxicology, the study of poisoning. Not only has the use of poison as a murder weapon declined almost to nothing over the last fifty years, but the investigation of drug action and the sophistication of analytical techniques have reached such a degree of complexity that forensic pathologists now readily hand over most problems to their colleagues in biochemistry and pharmacology.

Though homicidal poisoning has almost vanished in this country, its place has been more than adequately filled by three other problems. These are suicides, accidental poisoning in children and toxic hazards of industry.

Toxicology is a vast subject, and no more than mere scratching of the surface can be attempted here. However, some aspects of the forensic pathology of poisoning are common to all those toxic agents seen in routine examination of fatal cases.

Firstly, the actual diagnosis of death from poison can be difficult in the extreme, especially when there is no history to suggest the possibility before autopsy. A death from, say, a head injury needs no history for attention to be draw n to it, but this is not necessarily so in toxic deaths. Many poisons leave no external or internal signs, and unless the fact or suspicion of poisoning is evident from the circumstances, then even the best post-mortem examination may miss the real cause of death. This is cold comfort for would-be murderers by poison, as those substances usually used by killers *do* leave signs or cause symptoms before death. The poisons that leave very little evidence in the body are usually so repugnant that hardly any method, however ingenious, could persuade the victim to swallow them. One of the many situations in novels and films that is guaranteed to send a forensic pathologist into hysterics, is the common one of sleeping tablets being dropped surreptitiously into the victim's coffee or whisky — in real life the drug would not dissolve without considerable effort, but more important, would taste so awful that it would be spat across the room and not sipped with the usual appearance of enjoyment on the actor's face!

Returning to the missed poisoning at autopsy, where no circumstantial suspicion of poisoning exists and the deceased has some natural disease sufficient to account for death (as is extremely common in older people, who very often have enough coronary artery disease to satisfy the pathologist), then the poisoning may well be missed.

The only way to avoid this is to perform routine screening for poisons on every autopsy, no matter from what cause they appeared to die. This at once raises a major question — for what poisons is the analyst to search and how is a limit fixed upon the amount of investigation to be carried out? Unless one knows what sort of poison to look for, the analysis could take weeks and cost hundreds of pounds — even then, certain unusual substances might escape detection. Admittedly, the usual range of poisons is limited, but even so, routine analysis on all sudden deaths in the country would be an intolerable load on toxicological laboratory facilities and a quite unacceptable financial burden to be met from the coroner's fund, which comes from local authority taxation. It is certain that the ratepayer would not welcome an increase in his rates just to pick up a few unsuspected suicides each year, which is all that would be achieved. Some pilot studies of screening large series of routine post-mortems have been carried out, both in London and Denmark, and — though a number of surprising facts emerged, mainly about the incidence of hidden suicide — no unexpected homicide was detected. The overall gain, though commendable from a statistical point of view, would certainly not justify the cost of the present system of analysis. This is not to say that if an adequate national forensic medicine service were to be set up with built-in analytical facilities, it would not be useful and welcome.

Where no definite hint of poisoning is available before autopsy, it may be at least thought of in several types of case which come to the coroner's pathologist. If a previously healthy young person, especially a small child, is suddenly taken ill — more particularly if it has suffered sickness or bowel upset or is in coma, then accidental poisoning is high on the list of possibilities. Small children are especially at risk from household and garden substances. The list of dangerous things is limitless, but the main offenders are medicines left around the house and chemicals from the cleaning cupboards, garage and garden shed. Poisonous plants are another source, though these usually cause illness rather than death.

Accidental domestic poisoning in children has reached such alarming proportions that publicity campaigns by poster and in newspapers have been launched. Methods have been sought to make pill-boxes 'child-proof' by special lids that require some trick to remove them, though cost has been against the success of this precaution. Many of the drugs prescribed for adults are highly-coloured and sugar-coated, making them very attractive to small children. Indeed, quite a number of tablets and capsules are indistinguishable from some popular brands of sweets, and this fact has contributed to many fatalities.

The main offenders amongst the medicines left lying around the house are mother's iron tablets and grannie's sleeping capsules. Instead of being locked away in a medicine cupboard (now available with hidden child-proof locks) they are left on bedside tables, kitchen drawers and worst place of all, the bathroom cabinet. Another dangerous spot is the cupboard under the sink, where disinfectants, bleaches and chemical cleaners are on display at ground level, easily accessible to inquisitive toddlers or crawlers. In the garage and garden shed are weedkillers, insecticides, paint removers, antifreeze and a score of chemicals freely available in the shops, but potentially as lethal to a child as a loaded gun. When such a case comes to him, the pathologist is at his most sensitive, as surely these must be the most tragic cases of all, w here young lives are lost through nothing more than unthinking carelessness.

Numerically, suicide accounts for the vast majority of fatal poisonings in this country, mainly because coal-gas and barbiturates are the favourite means of self-destruction. In a recent year, there were 1803 suicides from barbiturates alone, compared with 1702 from coal gas; accidental deaths from coal gas amounted to 824 in the same period.

The very few homicidal poisonings are inflated by the tragic 'mother murders' where a woman commits suicide by coal-gas and takes her children with her. In the year quoted, 1967, murder by poisoning accounted for 25 deaths.

Industrial and agricultural poisoning fatalities are by no means uncommon and again the range of substances is vast — and increasing all the time with the expansion of industrial methods. The most powerful insecticides have caused many deaths, more so on the continent than in Britain. Parathion and similar substances containing organic phosphorus are the main culprits. They are related to war gases and very minute doses can cause death. Another large group are the chlorinated hydrocarbon insecticides, though these more often cause illness rather than death. The effects of these compounds on the animal life of the world is now becoming a vast problem, but acute poisoning in man has been with us for some years.

In industry, workers are exposed to all sorts of poisons, and a special department of the Factory Inspectorate has medical officers whose job it is to detect and prevent health hazards such as these. Gases of all sorts, heavy metals like lead and mercury and organic chemicals, all with either short or long-term toxic effects, are a mere fraction of the dangerous substances that can be met with in industry.

Though well outside the province of the pathologist, a mention of treatment of poisoning may be made. There is a common misconception that every poison has an 'antidote' — nothing could be further from the truth, and in fact the number of true antidotes to the enormous range of common poisons can be counted on the fingers. Treatment consists of removing the remaining poison, by stomach wash-outs, fresh air etc., then supporting life by helping breathing, heart action and general medical care.

The main object is to keep the patient alive while his own body deals with the poison, and in recent years great advances in mechanical respirators, artificial kidney machines and resuscitation generally have greatly improved the outlook in acute poisoning. Poisoning has reached such a degree as to be a major part of medical care; it was recently estimated that no less than one in every seven admissions to a large hospital in Britain was for deliberate self-poisoning (even excluding accidents!). Poisons information centres have been set up in most large cities, with a twenty-four-hour telephone advisory service on identification of poisons and best methods of treatment.

Though, thankfully, the pathologist once again sees only the tip of the ubiquitous iceberg; the problem in the community is vast. CARBON MONOXIDE POISONING

The heading could almost be 'coal gas poisoning', but for a few cases of incomplete combustion fatalities and some industrial accidents due to escape of this gas. Apart from these, the domestic gas supply is the commonest single source of fatal poisoning in these islands, though sleeping tablets now run it a close second.

Coal gas is a variable mixture of several sorts of combustible gases, obtained from coking plants, blast furnances etc. and lately from oil refineries and, of course, natural gas from the North Sea.

The proportion of carbon monoxide varies from place to place and in the same supply from time to time. It usually lies in the range of 5 to 20 per cent, the rest being made up by methane, hydrogen etc. North Sea gas contains no carbon monoxide.

The danger of carbon monoxide lies in its great affinity for haemoglobin, the red constituent of blood cells. It has a binding power for haemoglobin over 200 times greater than oxygen, and when combined it prevents the access of oxygen to the red cells. So it is not a poison in the accepted sense, but rather an internal asphyxiant. As carbon monoxide is so much more keen on the red cell pigment than oxygen, small concentrations can build up to a toxic level, the speed with which this is done depending on the proportion of the gas in the atmosphere. Even people who work in heavy traffic, like policemen, can accumulate enough to cause minor symptoms of headache; all town dwellers and cigarette smokers have a small quantity in their blood.

Though suicides account for the great majority of fatalities from this substance, the rate of increase of accidental deaths has become alarming. They rose from 345 in 1940 to 540 in 1967. This is one sector where the introduction of a carbon monoxide-free natural gas supply will be of benefit. It wras found in Basle some years ago that on a change-over to natural gas, the number of suicides in the city remained the same, as people used some other method when gas was denied them, but the accident rate fell dramatically, especially amongst old people. It is the elderly who are particularly at risk from coal gas. Often living alone, frequently slow and forgetful, and much addicted to boiling kettles for cups of tea, they start to light the gas stove, turn on the supply, forget the matches and then sit down for a rest and fall asleep. They allow7 kettles and saucepans to boil over and put out the flame; their sense of smell has gone, their gas appliances are often neglected and unsafe and because of these and other factors they are very prone to this form of poisoning. Old people are also much more sensitive to the substance; whereas a healthy young adult needs a 50 to 60 per cent saturation of his blood to die, senile victims are frequently discovered to have only 20 or 30 per cent combined with their haemoglobin.

The coal gas suicide usually employs an oven or gas-ring to end his or her life. The pattern is typical and some suicides go to great trouble to protect other people, erecting "Danger — Gas" signs on their doors, which like the windows are often sealed. The victim usually makes himself comfortable, placing cushions on the floor or leading a long pipe to the bed. The head is often covered by a blanket into which the pipe is led, or a plastic bag with the pipe fixed into it is used. All these signs become very familiar to the forensic pathologist, and very rarely does a murderer try to imitate the scene.

In the panic following a murder, futile attempts may be made to simulate a suicide. A headmaster of a secondary school in a small Northern town had been having an affair with the gym mistress for some time. His wife discovered a large sum of money that he had withdrawn for a weekend with his mistress. She threw this on to the fire and the husband inflicted fatal injuries to her head with a heavy carving knife. In spite of the fact that the kitchen where this occurred was covered in blood from floor to ceiling, he arranged cushions in front of the gas oven and attempted to drag the wife into a suicide pose. The limp body failed to stay with the head in the oven, and eventually the husband went upstairs to make a futile attempt at his own suicide by cutting his wrists.

Exhaust gases of a motor vehicle are occasionally used for self-destruction, as they contain about 6 per cent carbon monoxide or even more if the engine is faulty. The suicide either sits in the car with the garage doors closed or brings a pipe from the exhaust to the inside. The atmosphere of a small garage can develop a lethal concentration within a few minutes if a 2-litre engine is run with all ventilation stopped up. Some accidental deaths have occurred in this way.

The other domestic source of carbon monoxide poisoning is the incomplete combustion of various substances. This can occur in fires involving the house, where combustibles such as bedclothes, upholstery, furniture and woodwork smoulder in an oxygen-deficient atmosphere and produce large volumes of carbon monoxide. In fact, many deaths in conflagrations are due partly or wholly to poisoning with the gas and not to burns. It may also account for the failure of some people to escape from burning houses, as they may have already been rendered unconscious. Many cases occur where drunken people go to bed with a lighted cigarette, fall into an inebriated slumber, drop the cigarette into the bed and die from carbon monoxide poisoning with only minor or even no burns at all.

Another source of accidental poisoning is the defective gas geyser, especially in bathrooms. Here the production of monoxide is not directly from the gas supply, but from the incomplete combustion of the fuel. A common cause is blockage of the flue, either from ill-advised attempts at draught prevention, birds' nests in the outer pipe or some defect in the apparatus. Whatever the cause, it is an additional one to make the bathroom the most dangerous place in the house! Gas risks, electrocution dangers from dampness and excellent earthing, a slippery floor on which to fracture legs, and a cabinet-full of unused medicines, to say nothing of the risks of drowning in the bath!

The recognition of carbon monoxide poisoning is relatively easy, a welcome change from most of the problems of the pathologist. Though in most cases which come to him, there is a clear or at least a suggestive history — suicide notes, sealed rooms, smell of gas or obvious gas escape — in a proportion of cases, put as high as 20 per cent in accidental poisoning, there is no previous indication that the death may be due to gassing.

The most obvious feature at the autopsy is the cherry-pink colour of the skin, especially in the areas of dependent lividity. This can be immediately diagnostic if the saturation of the blood is high. It must be distinguished from the bright pink of oxyhaemoglobin prominent in bodies subject to low temperatures — these are seen in exposure cases, some drowning or even to mere storage in the refrigerator. The pink of cyanide poisoning tends to be a dusky purple, but might be confused in certain lights. Where the amount of monoxide is low, as is common in old people, then a 'snap' diagnosis is difficult or impossible. On internal examination the colour of the blood, organs and muscles may be obviously cherry-pink, but the only definite test is a spectroscopic or even chemical test of a blood sample.

The first method is most often used. It depends on the presence of black absorption bands present in the spectrum when light is passed through a dilute solution of blood and then through a prism. The rainbow of colours contains two dark bands, which are in different places for oxy-haemoglobin and for carboxy-haemoglobin. The amount of shift between the two positions can be measured and is an approximate indication of the percentage of the haemoglobin saturated by carbon monoxide.

In rapid deaths from the gas, little else can be found in the body at autopsy. Where recovery has occurred from partial poisoning, severe nerve and mental changes can occur.

Unsuspected accidental deaths are quite common, and occasionally even suicides are first detected at autopsy. If routine spectroscopy is carried out on all cases reported to the coroner, quite a few surprises are found, though this applies to all types of poisoning.

Circumstances which suggest carbon monoxide poisoning may be due solely to lack of oxygen. On a cold winter's morning on Tyneside an elderly woman and her adult son were found dead in an average sized room, every crack of which had been sealed against draughts. There was a gas fire with no proper flue. This was unlit and no gas was issuing. There was no gas in the room and examination of the bodies revealed no carbon monoxide. It was surmised that the fire and the occupants had used up all the available oxygen and that both fire and occupants had then expired.

SLEEPING DRUGS AND TRANQUILLISERS

Close on the heels of carbon monoxide as the most common poison come the drugs which act primarily on the brain. Until a few years ago, the drugs which caused death most often in adult suicides were the hypnotics (drugs to induce sleep) and the majority of these consisted of barbiturates of many kinds.

These are still the most dangerous of the group, but recently large numbers of another type of medication which acts on the nervous system has appeared. These are the 'tranquillisers', the modern prop against the stresses of civilisation. Though far less toxic than barbiturates — virtually innocuous, according to some claims of their manufacturers — they are prescribed in vast quantities and consumed by the ioo ton each year. Amid all this profuse medication, there are numerous cases of fatal overdose, almost all suicidal. Though they may be relatively safe, the operative word is 'relative', as enough of almost anything can kill you!

Barbiturates remain the most dangerous of the freely available drugs — for, though obtainable only on prescription and though controlled by the Poisons Act, there are so many distributed throughout the population that access is easy, especially to a determined suicide. For determined they can be — many inquests bring out a tale of hoarded capsules, stolen or borrowed drugs and all kinds of devices to obtain a fatal dose. The family doctor is often blamed, both in the press and by relatives or coroner in court, for prescribing too much at a time. In theory this is quite valid, but only a few days supply of the tablets may constitute a fatal dose, and both genuine patients and the doctor would suffer if prescribing became a bi-weekly event with each person. Naturally, where a patient exhibits depressive or frankly suicidal tendencies, then the supply should be carefully restricted and another responsible relative delegated to hand out the doses. But again, theory and practice diverge — such trends towards self-destruction are frequently submerged and the responsible relatives tend to melt away when most needed.

Other drugs commonly found in accidental or suicidal deaths are aspirin and the numerous proprietary pain-killers, most of which are freely available without prescription. Again, they are relatively safe, but sometimes enormous doses are taken by those intent on killing themselves. Deaths are not all that common when compared with the number of unsuccessful attempts (or *gestures*, which are not the same thing). Different individuals have vastly different tolerances to various drugs and this makes estimation of a minimum fatal dose virtually impossible. Aspirin is an example — survival has occurred after the taking of literally thousands of tablets, yet deaths have been reported (rarely) from an ordinary medicinal dose, where the unfortunate victim had some personal idiosyncrasy to the drug.

This individuality runs through the whole of toxicology and makes the interpretation very difficult for the pathologist or analyst. It is common for a coroner to ask the doctor for an opinion as to how much of the drug he thinks the deceased consumed. It was the practice until fairly recently, for a 'backwards' calculation of the number of tablets or capsules, using the analyst's report of the concentration in the blood and organs. This has been proved wrong with such consistency that it has reached a level of sheer guesswork. A *minimum* quantity can be roughly calculated, but variables such as destruction by the body, non-absorption from the stomach and intestine and tolerance to the drug make this a very precarious exercise. Probably the most honest thing the pathologist can do is to give his opinion whether or not the amount taken was greatly in excess of a medicinal dose. This is what the coroner wants to know in trying to make up his mind in those borderline cases which could be either an accident or a deliberate self-poisoning.

For some years many coroners and pathologists have perpetuated a convenient myth which has enabled them, in doubtful cases, to bring in a verdict of accident instead of suicide. They have suggested that a person taking a medicinal dose of a sleeping drug might become so muddled that they keep on taking further capsules or tablets (under the impression that they have not already swallowed the first dose) until a fatal level is reached. Though this rather naive explanation may be a kindness to some relatives and a way out where insurance or religious complications exist, it seems wrong that different standards should be applied at different times or in different places. Inquests on suicides should not be held at all, as they do no good and some harm, but while the law stands as it is, it should be uniform and not moulded for convenience or even patchy benevolence. The overworked tale of the forgetful pill-taker is just not acceptable. A minimum number of sleeping tablets that causes death is rarely less than half a dozen and usually a great deal more. One may conceive of a person taking the first, then another a short time later, from forgetfulness or torpor, but three, six or twenty is just not credible! A rapid acting barbiturate may produce drowsiness in twenty minutes and long before any type of barbiturate could build up a fatal level in small divided doses, the patient would be asleep and incapable of taking more.

Another well-known hazard of sleeping drugs is by no means a myth. This is the dangerous combination of alcohol and barbiturates. Both have a similar action, depressing the brain activity, including the nerve centres which control breathing. Overdose of either can cause death from this respiratory failure and hence the two taken together are even more potent. It was once thought that there was a 'multiplying' effect between them — that is, that the toxic action of both together was much greater than could be accounted for by mere addition of their effects. This is now known to be untrue and the danger is purely *additive* — but as long as the sum of the two reaches a certain level, then death is a possibility. After a heavy drinking bout, even a large normal dose of sleeping tablets can be really dangerous.

As far as the pathology of this sort of poisoning is concerned, things are more difficult than carbon monoxide. There is no colour change of the skin or tissues to give a clue and in many post-mortem examinations where sleeping tablets or similar drugs are suspected, absolutely nothing is found. This may be suspicious in itself, especially if the person is an otherwise apparently healthy person.

The usual pitfall of long-standing natural disease providing an obvious, but erroneous explanation is always present. In older people, especially men over 50, there is so often sufficient coronary artery disease to account for death, that unless routine screening for drugs or some suspicious circumstance is present, barbiturate cases will be missed.

Where a large dose has been consumed shortly before death — which can occur half an hour after swallowing, though it is usually much longer — then remains of the capsules or tablets may be found.

Many of the proprietary brands are brightly coloured, being blue, green, red, yellow or pink; this is especially so for the gelatine capsules, which rapidly dissolve when wet, releasing the white powder inside. If a large dose is taken masses of coloured, partly-dissolved gelatine may be found in the mouth, gullet or stomach. In other cases, there may be lumps of undissolved white powder or recognisable tablets surviving. Some drugs, like sodium amytal and aspirin, are irritative and may damage the lining of the gullet and stomach, leaving one of the few positive signs for the pathologist to see.

Where death has been slow, after perhaps many hours of coma, then the stomach may have emptied all the drug into the intestines where it is seldom recognisable. In these instances, chemical analysis is the only means of detecting an overdose. Even where visible remnants of excess tablets are present, the pathologist usually sends material from the autopsy for analysis, either to the nearest forensic laboratory or to a large hospital laboratory, if they are sufficiently equipped and experienced to carry out these very specialised tests. If there is any suspicion of criminal activity, then the samples will be taken over by the police and taken to the Home Office Laboratory.

The usual samples retained for analysis in this type of suspected poisoning include blood, urine, stomach contents and also the complete intestines and contents, as well as the liver, which is the organ which tends to accumulate the drugs whilst rendering them innocuous. The blood level is the most important single fact to be considered, as this reflects the concentration distributed in the body fluids at the time of death and can be roughly related to the level present in the brain, which is the important element in the causation of death. Barbiturates and similar poisons are detected and measured in the blood, and other samples by a technique known as 'spectrophotometry'. A clear extract is made of the drug and its absorption of ultra violet or infra-red radiation measured at different wavelengths: each drug has a special absorption pattern, recognisable to the analyst.

When attempting to calculate the total (or at least the minimum) amount that must have been taken by mouth, the concentration in the organs is important. The time of survival between taking the drug and death also matters, as the liver in its role as chemical factory of the body is constantly destroying the drug. When a person dies after prolonged coma, the blood level found at death may be far lower than it was some hours after swallowing the capsules.

All these matters shade off into the province of the biochemist and toxicologist — the specialist knowledge is so great and the rate of production of new drugs so rapid that the general forensic pathologist cannot pretend to be an expert as he was in the old days of the 'do it yourself' men.

POISONS GENERALLY ASSOCIATED WITH MURDER

Though rare now, homicidal poisonings contributed greatly to the classic murders of years ago. Far more arsenic and strychnine has been administered between the covers of detective novels than in real life, but when mild men and w omen disposed of their spouses or rivals by stealth, a few such selected substances were favoured.

Arsenic, the alleged weapon of Armstrong, Greenwood, Seddon and Marymont, was used for three main reasons. It was almost tasteless (an unusual and welcome attribute of a poison); it was fairly easy to obtain, being a common garden commodity; and it produced symptoms almost identical with natural disease of the bowel.

Even today, were arsenic to be used homicidally, very few doctors would suspect it on medical grounds. Most of the poisoners of the past have been discovered by events unrelated to the medical findings, such as peculiar domestic or financial circumstances, as well as unwise repetition of their activities within a short time. The corollary of this is that the wise poisoners have never been caught and so we do not know how many successes there have been — or still are!

The two most notorious murders by arsenic both took place in Wales almost within a year of each other — in both cases, a solicitor in a small country town was accused of poisoning his wife with arsenical weedkiller.

The first was the case of Harold Greenwood, tried at Carmarthen Assizes in 1920; he was alleged to have added arsenic to a bottle of burgundy. His wife died after a severe attack of vomiting and diarrhoea. The family doctor signed the death off as natural, but local gossip led to an exhumation ten months later. The body was found to exceptionally-well preserved and a minimum lethal dose of arsenic was found on analysis. Due mainly to the lack of motive and the smallness of the dose of poison, Greenwood was acquitted after a trial which attracted world-wide attention.

A short time later, at Hay-on-Wye in the adjacent county of Brecon, the other lawyer, Herbert Armstrong, lost his wife — and again, ten months later there was an exhumation, carried out this time by Bernard Spilsbury. The main reason for the exhumation was the suspicion of an astute general practitioner about an illness of another lawyer, who was Armstrong's business rival. An analysis of his urine revealed arsenic; a fantastic tale later emerged of chocolates being injected with weed-killer and of scones and sandwiches dosed with the same poison. Again, the body at exhumation was unusually well-preserved. The Director of Public Prosecutions, possibly smarting under his defeat in the Greenwood case, left no stone unturned to obtain cast-iron evidence this time, and Armstrong was convicted and hanged in 1922.

Arsenic can kill either by rapid acute poisoning with a single large dose or by the accumulation of insidiously small amounts typical of the chronic poisoning of the classic murderers. The first type is easily diagnosed at post-mortem (as long as the pathologist thinks of it) by the damage to the lining of the intestine and other features. Chronic poisoning may be spotted during life by an astute doctor, but again only if the possibility crosses his mind. Loss of weight, falling of hair, darkening of the skin and general sickness and bowel upsets may add up to a suspicious complex of symptoms. A doctor suspecting this is in a difficult position, and should either do nothing until he can get an analysis carried out under some pretext, or get the patient admitted to hospital, where rapid recovery and results of analyses may soon confirm any suspicions.

An interesting fact about chronic arsenic poisoning is that the substance is deposited in hairs during periods of administration. As the hair grows longer, a segment may contain arsenic and help to date the period during which the poison was given. Recent advances in analytical techniques can identify minute quantities, measured in millionths of a gram. The method was recently applied to some hairs from the body of Napoleon, as there has long been a suspicion that he was disposed of by his British captors with arsenic. The sample hairs were irradiated in an atomic pile, when heavy neutron bombardment converted the arsenic into a radio-active isotope, which could then be measured by its radio-active emission. The content of Napoleon's hair was found to be thirteen times the normal level, but the significance of this is not clear, as arsenic figured largely in many medicines of those times.

Another poison that has often appeared in murder cases (but far more frequently in suicide and accidents) is phosphorus. This was formerly used widely as a rat exterminator, until banned in 1963 on grounds of unnecessary cruelty. Several prosecutions for attempted murder by phosphorus have been brought in recent years: the attempts failed because of the obvious foul taste.

The list of poisons could be expanded almost indefinitely, and a new branch of pharmacology is growing up to study and explain the growing dangers of drug interaction, which is becoming more common as medication becomes more complex. Two drugs which might have no adverse effect when given singly, may react catastrophically when given together. As many hospital patients get an average of five to six different medicines (and up to twenty in some cases) the possible permutations are enormous, some of which may well be unpleasant, dangerous or even fatal. Though straying out of the field of the forensic pathologist, except where death results, this aspect of medicine is just one part of 'iatrogenic disease', a fancy description for the ever-widening field of sickness caused by medical treatment itself.

FIFTEEN — MEDICO-LEGAL MISCELLANEA

Forensic medicine, being such a diffused speciality, contains many topics that are hard to include within previous chapters. Some of these matters are pathological, and others administrative. The following selection gives some idea of the ramifications of the subject — indeed, any aspect of medicine or surgery acquires medico-legal implications whenever it comes in contact with civil liability, criminal action, ethical considerations or merely the administrative machinery of the State.

EXHUMATION

On rare occasions, bodies that have been buried with the proper legal formalities may have to be retrieved, either for further examination or, more commonly, for re-interment at some other site. This last reason applies when graveyards have to be disturbed for road works, building or even the flooding of ground for reservoir construction.

Where the body is to be re-examined, the decision to exhume is not taken lightly, and substantial evidence for its necessity must be submitted to the authorities, who consist of either the coroner for the area concerned or the Home Secretary.

If the subject of the desired exhumation had not previously been reported to the coroner at the time of death, then in theory the coroner alone can give permission for raising the body, if the reason is a further inquiry into the circumstances of the death. In practice, the coroner usually either requests the opinion of the Home Secretary or at least notifies him of the intention.

If the coroner has already held an inquest at the time of death, then his jurisdiction has expired and he has no power to authorise an exhumation. In this, and in any other case other than further enquiries about the death, the Home Secretary must give his permission.

The actual technique of exhumation depends on the probable nature of the death. A number of exhumations have been performed because of the suspicion of poisoning; in years gone by arsenic figured in several of these. Here considerable precautions had to be taken, including the collection of soil from around the coffin, as well as samples of coffin wood and grave clothes. This was to exclude any suggestion that arsenic found in the body could have seeped in from contaminating sources in the ground adjacent to the grave.

Exhumations were formerly done in macabre dramatic conditions in the middle of the night or before dawn, the autopsy being performed either on trestles at the graveside, behind canvas screens, or in some wretched gravedigger's hut in the corner of the cemetery. More enlightened conditions now prevail, and, though the coffin is usually raised at some early hour to avoid possible Press or public attention, the remains are taken by undertaker's van to a proper mortuary, where thorough examination can be conducted under relatively civilised conditions, with none of the furtive haste of the old 'cloak-and-dagger' days.

Whatever methods are used, identification of the remains is vital. Usually, a representative of church or local authority will identify the grave from a plan, and when the coffin is raised, the plaque on its lid must naturally be carefully checked.

The value of exhumation varies greatly with the time since burial, the season, the local conditions of the grave and, above all, with the nature of the examination required. A search for a relatively stable poison such as arsenic may be successful many years after burial, but it would be futile to expect any significant information in death from suspected morphine or other narcotic, after such a long time. Similarly, evidence of a fractured skull or other bony injuries may be evident decades — or even centuries — after death, but some soft tissue injury such as rupture of an abdominal organ from a blow, might have vanished within weeks in certain circumstances.

It is true to say, however, that such variation in decomposition can occur, that one is never safe in saying that exhumation would be useless, even after a period of months or years following burial, depending on what was being sought. The presence of adipocere or just simple delay in decomposition might provide some surprising results. The converse also occurs and complete dissolution of the body — and even skeleton — may occur in a short time in favourable conditions.

The procedure is usually much less objectionable than the lay person might expect. In fact, the longer the interment, the less unpleasant it is likely to be. The autopsy is carried out in the same way as usual. After many months, bruises, abrasions and most of the other signs of trauma may still be evident. In strangulation, fractures of the structures in the larynx may be found, as well as the usual signs in the soft tissues. The variables are so great that each case has to be evaluated separately and no firm forecast of the value of exhumation can be made.

Where homicide is concerned, many of the cases needing exhumation have been due to poison, for the obvious reason that these were the most likely to evade suspicion and enquiry in the first instance. A strangulation or stabbing is hardly likely to be missed — though there are extraordinary exceptions — and a police investigation or at least an initial autopsy and inquest would have been held. The poisoning exhumations have frequently arisen because of later attempts at a repetition of the deed, giving rise to retrospective suspicion and hence an exhumation.

SUDDEN DEATH FROM NATURAL DISEASE

On grounds of both importance and number, this topic really merits a whole chapter to itself — in fact, a whole book could be written on the various natural conditions which can give rise to sudden or unexpected death.

About 80 per cent of the autopsy load dealt with by pathologists on behalf of the coroners comes into this class. By far the greatest single cause of sudden death — and a leader in *all* forms of death, sudden or otherwise — is coronary artery disease. The incidence of death from this condition is creeping up remorselessly in 'civilised' countries (ones with a high standard of living and or nutrition). In England and Wales alone, the fatalities from 'coronaries' have now passed the 120,000 per annum mark, whilst in the United States they are well in excess of half a million per year, and climbing steadily.

This is no place to begin a dissertation on one of the biggest medical problems of the affluent society, but it can be said that some of the factors held to be responsible for this condition (one that was not even recognised until the early decades of this century!) are an over-adequate diet — especially of animal fats — lack of exercise and, less definable, the stresses of an urban society.

Another disturbing feature is not only the increase in total mortality, but the lowering of the age range in which death occurs. Though women seem virtually immune until after the 'change of life' men, who formerly were stricken in their fifties and sixties, now die increasingly often in their early forties and even thirties. Coronary artery disease has now reached almost epidemic proportions in 'executive' and professional men at the very time of their life when they are at the peak of their productivity and have the greatest family responsibilities.

The disease is part of a general degeneration of the arteries, where thickening of the lining and blockage of the channel of the vessel leads to deprivation of the blood supply to parts of the heart muscle. Though this degeneration goes on all over the body, it is frequently worst in the coronary arteries. The narrowing of the vessel predisposes to complete clotting of the residual channel — the common complication of 'coronary thrombosis', which leads to death of the heart muscle in the area supplied by the vessel.

Disease of the arteries causes most of the other types of sudden death, too — in fact, the old saying, 'A man is old as his arteries', is all too true. The aorta, the main blood-vessel coming out of the heart, may become thinned by this degenerative process, called 'atheroma' and may rupture, causing death by massive internal haemorrhage. Yet another frequent catastrophe is cerebral haemorrhage, contributed to by atheroma of the brain arteries. This either causes 'strokes' with paralysis or rapid death.

These arterial diseases account for the great majority of the natural deaths seen by the coroner's pathologist and make up about three-quarters of his total work-load. Apart from providing information enabling the coroner to dispose of the case, accurate statistics for the Registrar-General and data for research into the cause of this scourge, autopsy frequently assists in medico-legal aspects of coronary artery disease.

For instance, a road accident may have been caused by one vehicle going out of control for no apparent reason and smashing into another. Autopsy may reveal that the driver had had a recent coronary attack. Similarly, a driver about to be accused of the serious crime of causing death by dangerous driving, may be cleared by the finding that the pedestrian victim had just had some sudden natural disease like a 'stroke', which may well have caused him to collapse in front of the oncoming car. Scores of examples can be quoted from road and industrial deaths, where sudden natural diseases have a profound bearing on the interpretation of the case, which only autopsy can bring to light.

Questions of life insurance, expectation of life, and the contribution of natural disease to accidents have been resolved by pathological evidence. Many potential cases of manslaughter have been averted by the finding at post-mortem examination of some natural cause of death. This emphasises the fallacy of the argument of some coroners who dispense with autopsy in the 'obvious' case ... every case is a potential surprise and often questions of civil liability, insurance, etc., arise several years after the event, when it is then too late to get a pathologist's opinion.

BURNS

Burns are an all too common cause of death, especially in young children. There has been a terrible increase in the fatal accident rate from burns sustained in house fires during recent years, and once again, children and old people figure largely in this increase. Fatal scalding in baths and from overturned kettles and saucepans is again almost confined to young children.

The winter months are naturally the time of greatest hazard, when all forms of accessory heating are in use. It is an undoubted fact that paraffin heaters have contributed to this rise in accidents, though they are by no means the only culprits. Gas appliances have caused their share of fires, sometimes with an added explosion hazard, but faulty electrical wiring and open coal fires are frequent risks.

Cigarettes and matches constitute another source of danger, especially amongst the older victims, many of whom are either senile or intoxicated.

The pathology of fatal burns is often so appallingly gross that autopsy consists mainly of a description of the area involved — or even only of the surviving remnants. Yet there are a few important matters which must always be examined.

An elderly spinster in a Welsh village killed herself by sitting in a metal bath containing firewood, linoleum and paraffin and then igniting it. The upper part of the body became detached, fell on the floor and burnt its way through the boards, ending up in the basement below.

This localised burning of flooring has often been seen. A body may burn almost to nothing with only local ignition of carpet, flooring or a single piece of furniture. If a body burns near a source of draught, such as an open fireplace, then the body fat will supply sufficient fuel for complete destruction of the corpse with no general burning of the surroundings; this phenomenon led in less enlightened days to the term 'spontaneous combustion' being applied.

One of the prime objects is to confirm that death occurred *after* the burning and not before. Not a few murdered bodies have been disposed of by fire, in an attempt to disguise the foul play.

In the well-known 'Chalk Farm' murder of the thirties, the charred body of a man was found in a shed in a builder's yard. A suicide note written by Sam Furnace, the owner of the yard, was found and the body was assumed to be his. The coroner, Bentley Purchase, himself a doctor, was not satisfied with the circumstances and examined the body himself, finding a bullet hole in the back!

Laundry marks on remains of the shirt and, once again, dental evidence, established that the body was that of a young man, Spatchett, to whom Furnace owed money. Furnace had attempted the same deception as Rouse a couple of years earlier, that of substituting a murdered man for himself; as with Rouse, the forensic pathological evidence had soon shown that even a fierce fire cannot eradicate signs of identity.

Furnace was arrested in a Southend boarding house, but managed to commit suicide whilst in police custody by drinking hydrochloric acid.

To confirm that the victim was alive during the fire — though thankfully, this need not be synonymous with being conscious — the actual burns on the skin are inspected. If caused during life, there will almost always be a 'vital reaction' — a response of the tissues to severe heat, displayed by marked redness, which extends over a zone beyond the margin of damage, blisters and exudation of fluid. Post-mortem burns can mimic the redness and even the blisters, but there are differences which can be detected by the experienced eye.

If the body is so badly burned that destruction or carbonisation of the skin has occurred, things are more difficult. Internal examination may help to clarify the circumstances. A person in a house fire will have been exposed to dense smoke and soot particles, which come from smouldering bedding, fabric and furniture. These will be sucked down the air-passages and reach deeply into the lungs, if the person was breathing — that is, still alive. By the same process, the fumes will carry carbon monoxide into the lungs and hence into the blood, where it can be detected spectroscopically. Neither of these things can happen in a body burnt *after* death.

By taking blood samples for carbon monoxide estimation (also useful for alcohol analysis if there is a suspicion that the possibly drunken victim went to bed with a lighted cigarette) and pieces of lung for microscopic examination for soot, the pathologist can augment his naked eye opinion on this important question of the chronology of death.

ELECTROCUTION

Electrocution causes seventy to 100 deaths a year in this country. It is almost totally an accidental form of death, affecting two main groups of men — the 'do-it-yourself' home electrician and the industrial worker.

The greatest number of deaths are caused by the ordinary domestic supply of 240 volts alternating current. It is rather ironic that the alternation of fifty cycles per second is within the most dangerous range of all and that the voltage is also well in the lethal range, compared to the U.S. and Continental supply of no volts. It almost seems that Britain has deliberately chosen the most dangerous system available!

Death from electrocution is due to the passage of a current through the body, which paralyses either the muscles of breathing, or more often, the contractions of the heart. When breathing is affected, the outlook for recovery is better, as it has occurred following prolonged artificial respiration for as much as several hours.

Damage to the heart is usually immediately fatal, as the current causes the heart muscle to lose its normal rhythm and go into a useless twitching called 'fibrillation'.

The most dangerous pathway for the passage of a current is from the left arm to the feet, as this route crosses the axis of the heart; from arm to arm or from right arm to feet is also very dangerous. Shocks through a limb or even head have a much lower mortality.

The likelihood of death depends on the total current in milli-amperes that traverses the tissues. This in turn is dependent on the voltage, the resistance of the skin and the earthing facility at the exit point of the current. The latter is very important, and a fatal shock is virtually impossible from domestic supply if someone stands in rubber shoes on a carpet in an upstairs room (naturally assuming that no part of the body other than the feet is earthed). Unfortunately, many industrial or 'garden shed' electrocutions occur in damp conditions, on wet uncovered concrete floors. Working men's boots are often leather with metal nails in the soles, and most pathologists have seen exit burns on the soles of the feet coinciding with metal boot-studs.

The signs of electrocution may be very slight indeed. The entry of the current is usually on the fingers or hands, and the marks may be unnoticed by anyone but a pathologist. Two main types exist, the 'firm contact' and the 'spark burn'. The first is a blister, a wrinkle of skin containing a little fluid, which occurs when a firm grip is made on a live metal conductor. The spark burn may be very hard to find, merely a tiny pit or crust of yellowed skin, often with a pale halo around it where the shock has constricted the surrounding blood-vessels. These marks may be on the inside of fingers tightly clenched by rigor mortis and be very hard to find. Though earthing marks may be found on the feet, there is usually a diffuse exit through the damp soles which leaves no focal injury.

Internally, nothing is found except congestion due to lung or heart paralysis. There have been minute microscopical abnormalities described by research workers, but these are too subtle for the average pathologist to rely upon.

Very high voltage electrocution is sometimes seen in industry or amongst power-station or grid workers. Here burning is the main feature, and in fact many cases of survival from enormous voltages have been recorded, partly because the almost explosive results of the shock have thrown the workman clear. With domestic voltage, the arm muscles are frequently sent into spasm, so that the victim is unable to let go. This also constitutes a risk to any rescuer, who should insulate his hands before detaching the victim from the conductor.

Once again the bathroom is a black spot, as with carbon monoxide, drowning, poisons and falls. Damp conditions and perfect earthing via metal baths and waste pipes, makes it an electrical death trap. The proof of this is seen in the safety regulations, which prohibit power points in the bathroom and also insist on a cord ceiling-pull instead of the usual wall-switch for the light.

Even so, people defy these rules devised for their own safety and bring in electric fires, hair-dryers and other apparatus, so that every year, someone gets killed in his own bathroom.

POSTSCRIPT: MURDER, SUICIDE OR ACCIDENT?

In the foregoing chapters, much of the emphasis has been on the detection and investigation of violent deaths, often due to criminal action. It must be said again that in Britain, the emphasis on the latter is false, though other countries are less fortunate in their criminal death rates. In this context, a slight digression may be justified to put the present British homicide rate into the correct perspective compared to those abroad.

Exact comparisons are impossible, due to variations in distinguishing between murder, manslaughter etc. and in methods of record keeping, but a broad survey shows that Britain is happily near the bottom of the murder league.

Under most registration methods, causes of death are shown as the number per 100,000 population. The World Health Organisation keep global statistics, though these are slightly inflated by deaths due to operations of war being included in homicide. Thus under the W.H.O. classification, the rate of murder in Britain in 1967 was only 07 per 100,000. This gives an actual number of over 300 for England and Wales, which is approaching twice that recorded in Home Office figures, but even so a rate of 07 is very low.

Compare this with the United States, where the rate runs at about 6-o. In New York City alone, there are well over 1,000 murders a year, whereas in Britain, the total is around 150 for the whole country. Even the United States pales into insignificance contrasted to some other nations in the New World. The top of the league is vied for by Colombia and El Salvador, who have murder rates up to 36 per 100,000!

In Europe, there is a generally low rate, but even so some interesting differences are seen. Finland has the highest rate of about 2.3, closely followed by a quite different type of country, Bulgaria, with almost as much. The two lowest are Eire and Spain, which compete for lowest place with figures of around 0.1 to 0.3. It is a matter for speculation that the predominantly Roman Catholic countries tend to have the lowest homicide rates. The two already mentioned are the lowest in the world, and France and Italy have low average rates in spite of their expected fiery Latin temperament.

Even within the British Isles there is a definite variation in the frequency of murder. Eire, as we have seen, has virtually the lowest in the world. Northern Ireland has a slightly lower rate than England and Wales, but the balance within the United Kingdom is restored by Scotland which persistently has a significantly higher level, having easily the highest murder rate in Britain, almost all of the excess being contributed by the City of Glasgow.

Suicide is naturally far more common than murder in almost all countries except Latin America, where for example, in Colombia, murder is up to nine times more frequent than suicide! In Europe, again the Catholic lands have a very low rate, with Eire and Spain once more competing for bottom place, with only two or three suicides per 100,000. The U.K. has low European average at about 10, with much higher rates in Scandinavia, Austria, Czechoslovakia, Germany, Hungary and Switzerland. Far ahead of everyone else is West Berlin, with the prodigious rate of over 40! There must be truths of great importance to sociologists hidden in these figures. Why should France, a Roman Catholic country with a low murder rate, have a suicide rate of over 15?

The other member of the fatal trilogy that forms the title of this book is the accident. This category far outnumbers the other two in British death rates. About 40 out of every 100,000 die from some form of accident in Britain. Of these the largest number occur in the home and not, as might be expected, on the roads. Of these forty people, only about fifteen are road traffic fatalities, the rest — amounting to some 11,000 deaths — occurring mainly in domestic or industrial premises. Seven thousand road deaths is a very heavy toll, considerably greater than the number of suicides, yet the rate is almost double in Germany, Italy and the U.S.A. In the latter, over 50,000 lose their lives on the highways each year.

Returning to the more personal role of the forensic pathologist, we can see that the most important part of his contribution to the common good is not the detailed investigation of the relatively rare murder, but the much more frequent elimination of criminal interference in deaths due to accident, suicide and natural causes, which would otherwise occupy much police time and public expense. Added to this is the patient day-today collection of reliable causes of death in the community, which adds to the pyramid of medical knowledge that will eventually help in suppressing fatal diseases and man-made hazards.

In England and Wales, there are now over half a million deaths per year. More than one fifth of these are reported to the coroner and thus a large proportion of the deaths where the cause is not already known by clinical doctors are classified by pathologists — a considerable contribution to the sum total of medical knowledge concerning the factors that lead to death in our community.

The aspect which naturally catches the public eye in disproportionate degree is the criminal case. Though numerically the homicide investigation is of minor value in Britain, the deterrent value must not be under-estimated. In spite of recent criticisms and its admittedly cumbersome administration, the British medico-legal system ensures that homicide, unlike crimes against property, is not something that can easily be 'got away with'.

The rate of failed detection in this country is less than 10 per cent and the tight procedures of investigation — of which forensic pathology is a vital part — ensures that the wholesale mayhem existing in some countries of the New World is unlikely to develop here. In homicide, probably more than anything else, prevention is certainly better than cure!

What of the future? The staffing and financial difficulties at present besetting academic departments of forensic pathology have been mentioned in earlier chapters and it is a matter of some concern that the small band of devotees are becoming whittled away rapidly, as the older members retire and virtually no new pathologists enter to take their place. The Government, who are well aware of and willing to press ahead with reforms and developments in both the police service and the forensic science laboratories, steadfastly ignore the decay in forensic medicine. They lay the responsibility on the universities, who increasingly wish to shed the burden of what they consider to be a public service. On the technical side, no great revolution in methods is apparent, nor is it urgently needed, except in ever-widening field of toxicology and serology.

As always, the tools of the forensic pathologist remain his eyes, his hands and above all, his experience. No computer can replace the almost intuitive recognition of some tiny fact by a pathologist who has seen it before. Experience is something impossible to convey accurately in textbooks or even by the most perfect colour-photography. A forensic doctor may know' that what he is looking at means so-and-so, but may be unable to enumerate the points which make the decision definite, often to the exasperation of a lawyer in court. For example, a body with a swollen face due to decomposition developed in the face-down position after death, may have a black eye identical with that sustained from a blow, yet the pathologist who has seen half a dozen before, can immediately eliminate violence, without being able to write an essay on *why* he knows this. It may take a decade for a pathologist to reach this state of experience, which makes it all the more worrying to see the present generation of crime doctors getting so thin on the ground. Even if there was a miraculous influx of recruits tomorrow, it would be years before a reservoir of really experienced men was available.

Some technical advances are being made in this subject, though the rate of growth is probably slower than in any other medical speciality, with the exception of serology and toxicology. In these, the 'spin-off' of other sciences like immunology, biochemistry and pharmacology, assists in more rapid development and as far as toxicology is concerned, the almost explosive increase in the number of drugs in use makes such progress a vital necessity. In pathology itself, the main problems have long been the estimation of the time since death and the distinction of wounds inflicted *before* death from those made *after* death. In the latter problem, the use of enzymes has recently been of considerable importance. Professor Raekallio of Finland has pioneered methods for detecting wounds made shortly before death by the sudden burst of activity of enzymes, which prepare the tissues for the onset of healing of the wound. If the wound was made *after* death, naturally no such reaction would occur. These tests still require that the wound be inflicted at least one hour before life became extinct, and further research goes on to try to find methods which will detect this 'vital reaction' even nearer the actual moment of death.

A similar solution to a comparable problem has been found in the evaluation of sudden death from heart disease. Quite frequently, a fatal accident will occur in circumstances suggesting that the dead man suffered a heart attack immediately before the catastrophe. Even at post-mortem nothing may be found, due to the insufficient time for visible pathological changes to occur. The use of enzymes (the organic catalysts that help produce energy and growth in the body) may help to prove abnormal tissue conditions in the period immediately preceding death. This may have profound medicolegal implications in the field of civil or criminal responsibility as well as in such matters as life insurance and the presumption of survivorship in multiple fatalities.

It is in these relatively limited technical matters — apart from serology and toxicology — that advances in forensic pathology will be seen in coming years. Like all other specialities, there is an increasing tendency to fragmentation and super-specialisation. In spite of the impression gained from television fiction, the forensic pathologist no longer studies bullets or compares fibres from clothing. His contact with poisons is mainly confined to the collection of body fluids and organs for the expert non-medical analyst, though the difficult job of interpretation of the results is all too often thrown back to him! No longer does he test the group of blood stains in criminal cases — the ever increasing complexity of these techniques is carried out by expert serologists.

Yet the central core of his work remains, unpleasant and revolting to most people, carried out in uncomfortable surroundings, often in inferior premises and occasionally in frankly unhygienic conditions. For every case invested with spurious glamour by the newspapers, he conducts several hundred in obscurity, but the major part of his contribution to the welfare of the community depends on these repetitive, often monotonous and sordid tasks that must be amongst the least envied jobs in existence.

22395154R00116

Printed in Great Britain
by Amazon